"There is some danger that our idea of Pericles may be of a rather chilly and inhuman person. Even the Athenians of his own years of fame found him 'Olympian'; and from the superhuman to the inhuman is a short step in thought. In his own day he was respected and trusted as none other, but really loved only by a few, who have left no memorial. To this, his own character contributed. Self-effacing he was not; but one might coin the expression 'self-immersing.' Athens as he made her was not only his life-work but his most abiding passion, loved to the detriment both of his property and of his family life. It was, indeed, perhaps his most tragic limitation that Greece, apart from Athens, meant no more to him than Europe to most patriots of the present day; but few moderns can cast stones at him there. His business was her business, his recreation the devising of new mean of expression for Athenian art, song, athletics, and lyrical drama—that, and conversation with pioneer thinkers of his time on the physical or social sciences. His intimate friends included Sophocles, Pheidias, Anaxagoras the scientist, Damon the musician; the woman he loved was one whose intelligence was respected by Socrates. As a young man he was a soldier of conspicuous gallantry. He had also a dry, ironical humour. . . . Olympian to the outside world he may have been, but chilly —no. Even in Athens, no man lived more fully than Pericles."

—*From the Introduction*

Men and History
Collier Books Ready or in preparation

Pericles and Athens

A. R. BURN

SENIOR LECTURER IN ANCIENT HISTORY
AT THE UNIVERSITY OF GLASGOW

COLLIER BOOKS New York

First Collier Books Edition 1962

Second Printing 1966

Pericles and Athens *was published in a hardcover edition by the Macmillan Company.*

This title first appeared as a volume in the Teach Yourself History series under the general editorship of A. L. Rowse.

The Macmillan Company, New York

Author's Note

MY MOST hearty thanks are due to Professor A. W. Gomme and Mr. R. H. Dundas, both of whom read this book in typescript (Mr. Dundas also in proof) and gave me the benefit of their great knowledge of fifth-century Athens. If I have occasionally ventured to differ from them, it is at my own risk. I wish also to thank Professor H. T. Wade-Gery for his kind answers to questions; some of my debts to his published work are indicated in the text. Lastly but not least I thank my wife for a great share in much of the incidental drudgery of book-making, and for her unfailingly lucid answers to requests for criticism on many details.

NOTE TO THIRD IMPRESSION

In this impression the Note on Books (pp. 209ff.) has been brought up to date, and some minor corrections have been made in the text.

A. R. BURN.

GLASGOW, 1960

TO

AIGLI AND PANDORA AND THEOPHANO

THE ATHENIANS

Favor comes to a man because, for a brief moment in the great space of human change and progress, some general human purpose finds in him a satisfactory embodiment.

F. D. ROOSEVELT.

November, 1932

Contents

Part IV / **The Last Crisis**

Introduction

(i) The Background

IN THE MIDDLE of the Plain of Athens—a typical Greek plain, formed of the alluvium brought down by the rivulets Kephisos, Ilisos, and Eridanos[1] from the surrounding hills—a miniature range of rocky hillocks breaks the surface. Highest of them is the spike of Lykabettos, from which you may look over the whole Saronic Gulf to the coast and mountains of the Peloponnese; even on a clear day pick out the citadel of Corinth, some fifty miles away. But of greater interest to early man was a lower rock, with steep sides for defence, space on top for habitation, and copious springs under the rocks, where water could be got without far to venture or far to carry.

The rock was not yet so flat-topped or so precipitous as it is to-day. Its present shape is due to works of building and revetment performed when Pericles was a youth. But already it was an almost ideal citadel when Neolithic men first settled there and made of it their "High City," the Acropolis.

With such a refuge from which to till the good land round about, and the sea at Phaleron far enough away to deter casual sea-raiders, Athens prospered. During the

[1] Names that have become virtually English words are spelt in the most familiar manner, e.g. Pericles, Æschylus, Piræus; other names, as in Greek, not as in Latin, e.g. Kimon, Leagros, not Cimon, Leagrus; Thucydides (historian), but Thoukydides, son of Melêsias.

The circumflex (^) is used to indicate syllables that were long in ancient Greek, except final -és, -on (in men's names), -as and -e, which were always long, and vowels long by position, i.e. followed by two or more consonants.

A, E, I and O were probably pronounced in ancient Greek more or less as in modern French or Italian; Y like French U; AI like I in NINE; EI as in REIN; OU as in ROUTE; G always hard; CH as in LOCH. A "plain English" pronunciation—Pericles rhyming with "these," Kleinias with "tiny ass," and CH pronounced as in CHORD —is, however, time-honoured.

Bronze Age there were still many other similar "cities" scattered over the land of Attica; but after being violently introduced to wider horizons by the late Bronze Age imperialism of Crete, the settlements drew together, forming at last one centralised state of Attica, with Athens its capital; thanks, men said, to the wise statesmanship of Theseus, the same who built ships secretly in Troizen, across the gulf, and carried out a raid of revenge on Crete, after the last King Minos had fallen in Sicily.

The early Iron Age which followed was a time of storm and stress, with the crash of the Bronze Age monarchies and the immigration of rough Dorian tribes from the north. But even in this age Athens was relatively fortunate. The main migration came down through Western Greece. The little cities and thin-soiled peninsula of Attica roused no such violent cupidity as the treasures of Mycenæ or the rich plain of Thebes; and though crowded with "displaced persons" from the broken kingdoms of the Peloponnese, Attica, not without fighting, survived unconquered.

The refugees, or most of them, passed on to found new cities on the west coast of Asia Minor, though some remained and intermarried with the people of the land; and while in the following centuries other parts of the Greek world suffered from race-feuds, over-crowding, or the growing-pains of new communities, the Athenians, with their comparatively spacious territory and homogeneous "Ionian" population, were happy enough for a time to have little history.

Dorian Corinth and Megara on the isthmus, Ionian Chalkis in Euboia, Miletos and other cities in Ionia, having become stabilised after the great migrations, began again, before 700 B.C., to pour out a surplus population to Italy and Sicily, to the north Ægean, and later even to the Black Sea. This colonising movement ultimately upset the aristocratic governments, under which most of the cities had settled down after the turmoil; for colonisation led to a great growth of trade, between colonies sited with an eye to good corn-land and mother-cities in the rocky Ægean world, where the population still continued to

grow. Hence arose new social groups and types: the
parvenu rich trader and sea-captain; the noble turned
capitalist, richer, more magnificent and also greedier than
his farming ancestors; the impoverished noble, unsuccessful in the new age; and especially the sailors and town
workmen, less tractable and disposed to obey their "betters" than the old-time peasant; uprooted men, concentrated together in the growing towns, and "ill to persuade," as the Greeks said, if only because, when times
were bad, the peasant could tighten his belt and survive, but the town worker was in immediate danger of
starvation.

The result naturally was a wave of revolutions. In state
after state, during the seventh century, in those parts of
Greece affected by the commercial revolution, the hungry
and the dispossessed found a leader—usually a nobleman,
disinherited or merely ambitious—to overthrow the aristocracy by armed force, and redress so far as in him lay the
wrongs of his supporters.

These leaders were the "tyrants," a native word from
Asia Minor meaning "despot" or, as we now say, "dic-
tator." The sinister sense of the word appears only in a
later age, when the tyrants had outlived their usefulness.
They were revolutionary leaders, often popular, but emphatically not democratic—though by breaking up the
aristocracies they paved the way for the more liberal republics that followed.

Such was the historical background of classical Greece.

Athens followed, generally speaking, the common pattern of the progressive and commercial states; but she followed it with a difference. At Athens, as elsewhere, the
nobles and squires had reduced the old monarchy to a
cipher and established their control of the government,
through a "Regent" or Archon, elected at first for life or
for a long term, later for one year; but at this stage
Athens stopped for some time. In the thousand square
miles of Attica—much more of a "country" than the territories of most Greek city-states—there was for a long
time room for all.

Attica sent out no colonies. Nevertheless, the new age

of commerce and oversea contacts, east and west, did not leave her unaffected. In the late seventh and the sixth century we find successively a premature and abortive attempt at a tyranny; reforms aiming at averting such a catastrophe (publication of the laws by one Drakon, and later a cancellation of peasant debts by Solon); and at last, after the tyrants of Corinth and Megara had already fallen, a tyranny at Athens. But there is something significant even in this very lateness of Athenian development.

The wide area of the country, which made colonisation unnecessary and so slowed up constitutional progress, helped to support an enormous population for a Greek state; at its highest point, in Pericles' time, probably over 250,000 Athenians, in addition to many thousands of free non-citizens, and at least 100,000—probably nearer 200,000—slaves. Significant, too, is the lack of bitterness in the Athenian internal strife. Class-struggles at Athens were not exacerbated by a conquest as in the Dorian states; and though bitter enough, yet in old and tradition-ridden Attica, even in the revolutionary period, they never led to atrocities as in Dorian Megara or half-Asiatic Miletos. The crowning success of continuity and moderation at Athens comes after the triumph of democracy, in the lifetime of Pericles, in the fact that most (though not all) of the old families accepted and worked the democratic constitution; a fact of which Pericles himself is the most conspicuous example.

Athens in her prime, then, had a population surpassing that of any other Greek state, and an internal solidarity unmatched in the history of that politically all too active people. One state had an even larger territory: Dorian Sparta, owning the southern two-fifths of the Peloponnese, and controlling the rest of it through a system of alliances. But in Sparta's territory the vast majority of the people were either free but unenfranchised farmers of the provincial villages, or serfs—the Helots—often bitterly hostile to their lords. This was especially so in the western territory of Messenia, which Sparta had conquered just at the time when other states were expanding oversea.

Sparta's potentially great strength was usually paralysed by her internal conflicts; and in the heyday of ancient Greece the question whether the nation would achieve political unity meant in effect whether it would achieve it under the forceful leadership of Athens.

Greece failed to achieve unity, as modern Europe appears to be failing. Athens, under leaders of whom Pericles was the greatest, tried to impose unity by force, and broke herself in the attempt. That is the Athenian tragedy.

It remains to say something about the sources of our all too scanty knowledge of the great Athenian and his times.

(ii) Pericles and Plutarch

It is surprising how scanty those sources are.

There is, of course, the *Life* by Plutarch; a pleasant, readable, fifty-page essay by a country gentleman and scholar, who lived, it is true, over five hundred years later, but who had access to the whole body of ancient Greek literature, most of which is now lost. Plutarch quotes, in this essay alone, some twenty authorities, including eight contemporaries (three prose-writers and five writers of topical comedy). Of these eight we have only Thucydides, whose *History of the Peloponnesian War* begins in earnest four years before Pericles' death, after a brief historical introduction, and a few comedies of Aristophanes.

Of later historical writing on this age, we have only Plutarch himself, the muddle-headed, scissors-and-paste *Universal History* of Diodoros the Sicilian, and the short history of the *Athenian Constitution* commonly known (e.g. to Plutarch) as Aristotle's; though it contains so much shallow thinking and so many demonstrable blunders as to suggest the gravest doubts whether it can be by the great man himself.

By way of additional "background" material, we have the findings of archæology, especially of inscriptions; thanks now especially to the American excavators of central Athens and to two great American epigraphists, B. D. Meritt and the late A.B. West, who, with Professor Wade-Gery of Oxford, have carried on the earlier work of a line of great German scholars. The Greek practice of inscribing their most important public documents on stone results in our having, despite the depredations of later builders and burners of marble for lime, considerable fragments of the public records of Athens—something like the proportion that one might recover from a rather badly bombed record office to-day. It may also be taken as certain that what remains to be discovered is much less than what is now known. To these documents we shall have occasion to refer frequently.

But for biographical material, Plutarch, the author of the only surviving ancient book on Pericles, remains the chief source. Moreover, through the translations of Florio and North and their numerous followers, he has been, ever since the Renaissance, probably the most read of all Greek historical writers, and has set the tone for much ordinary, educated, non-specialist opinion on the ancient world. It is therefore necessary to begin with a warning.

If we compare Plutarch's and Thucydides' accounts of the events leading up to the "world war"—the only crisis in Pericles' life for which we have this great contemporary writer as a "control"—we find, not merely difference of emphasis, which would be natural as between a biographer and a sternly scientific historian, but *incompatibility*. Plutarch mentions, with reserve, a theory which several modern writers have adopted whole-heartedly, that Pericles at the end of his life deliberately involved his country in a war, because his political position was being dangerously attacked through prosecutions of his friends, and he thought a war would divert people's attention from certain deficiencies in his own accounts. In support of this he quotes some lines of Aristophanes, who was living at the time. If, however, we refer to Thucydides, we find not only no mention of this alleged reason for Pericles heading the war-party (*that* might be merely a case of our austere historian ignoring personal details); we find explicit statements—all the more convincing for being quite casual, not violent protestations—that Pericles was the most influential political leader in Athens at the time, so that the enemy, "considering that Athens would be easier to deal with if he were eliminated," made vigorous but unsuccessful attempts to shake his position by propaganda.

What, then, of Aristophanes?

That Aristophanes was writing comedy need not discredit him; many a true word is spoken in jest. But if we look up Aristophanes' own plays, we find that when the hero states this theory, his hearers answer: "Well, we never heard *that* before." Evidently, years after the event, the idea was still a novelty; which, among a nation of born gossips, is conclusive evidence that it cannot be taken seriously.

Evidently Plutarch—an essayist, not an historian, as he himself reminds us—was sometimes a little guileless in the use of his sources. He is capable of rejecting such wild stories as that Pericles in youth procured the assassination of his own party-leader in order to succeed him, and in later years seduced his son's wife and poisoned his friend Pheidias in prison in order to suppress his evidence. Such tales, he realises, are incompatible with the respect in which Pericles was generally held by serious people—for instance, by Plato, who knew scores of people who remembered Pericles, and admired the man though he disliked his politics. But Plutarch is an author who needs to be used with great care. He is widely read, but not scientific-minded. When faced with a conflict of evidence he is inclined to count heads, without asking himself if one witness is better than another. Also, his idea of a biography is chiefly a character-sketch. The hero's birth comes at the beginning and his death at the end, but in between, events may be given in almost any order, "to point a moral and adorn a tale." Plutarch was not an historian and—he has many sympathisers—could not be bothered with dates.

Also, the picture given in Plutarch's *Pericles* is essentially a picture of the "elder statesman," in the last twenty years of his life. Athenian prose literature had scarcely started its career when Pericles died (in Ionia, it went back farther); and when historians in the next century drew on oral traditions, these traditions were naturally the reminiscences chiefly of men who were still young when Pericles was sixty. We have no first-hand glimpses of the young Pericles at all. (For one thing, he was evidently a "good" boy, and did not give rise to amusing stories of early wildness.) We do not even know the year of his birth. Plutarch consequently found that all his authorities always pictured Pericles as the leading man in Athens. The real reason for this was that even comedies do not seem to have been written down and kept, until Pericles was already about forty-five; but Plutarch naïvely pictures him as already the acknowledged leader of the Athenian democrats from the very start of his political career.

Pericles' life is thus very thinly documented except in his last twenty years, for which we have a fair number of allusions from comedies, stories handed down by his younger contemporaries, and so on. It is relatively well-documented only for his last four years, for which we have Thucydides.

And one further warning: when the sources available to Plutarch did give personal detail about Pericles, they tended to be hostile.

Athenian comedy had to caricature. It could, after all, hardly be funny otherwise; in any case, personal abuse "for luck" was part of its old agrarian magical *raison d'être*. With the earliest prose writers the reason was more serious. First, they were, like most Greek writers, members of a leisured class, and usually anti-democratic. Secondly, Attic prose literature (apart from speeches) starts as a literature of reflection and criticism in a world gone wrong. Hence, apart from Thucydides—the only great Greek thinker to write of him from personal acquaintance—there is a strong tendency to hostility towards the man who had led Athens in the direction in which she had gone. It appears both in Plato and in Aristotle; and apparently it was strong among the fourth-century historians, now lost, whom Plutarch knew well.

Lastly, the two *contemporary* prose writers, other than Thucydides, whom Plutarch quotes were both non-Athenians, and both, probably, hostile to Athenian imperialism. This is certainly true of the more forcible of the two, the pamphleteer Stesimbrotos, from the island of Thasos, which Athens had subdued; a resident in Athens but violently hostile, it seems, to all Athenians except the small reactionary clique, who promised freedom to all "allies" if once they gained power. The other writer, Ion of Chios, a tragedian who also wrote memoirs, is a man of whom we would gladly know more; but his work, less pungent than that of Stesimbrotos, seems to have left less impression on the tradition. Stesimbrotos is the chief source for those gems of obloquy which Plutarch rejects. That he is right goes without saying. Athens loved (and loves) a good scandal; but a man about whom such stories were even plausible could never have held a unique position of trust and influence for many years. And that he did hold such a position, even the comic poets testify; their usual nickname for him was God Almighty—"the Olympian Zeus."

It is our great loss, then, that even Plutarch had, as sources on Pericles the man, only comedy, which caricatured, or political writing, mainly hostile, or the tradition of the next century based on memories of old men, who were young when Pericles was already the "prime minister." Pericles wrote nothing; and no one who knew him really well wrote a memoir of him. The tradition of him is rather like the physical portrait that forms our frontispiece, based on Roman copies of an idealising bust—for in Pericles' time realistic portaiture, like prose, was still undeveloped.

In the circumstances, there is some danger that our idea of Pericles may be of a rather chilly and inhuman person. Even the Athenians of his own years of fame found him "Olympian"; and from the superhuman to the inhuman is a short step in thought. In his own day he was respected and trusted as none other, but really loved only by a few, who have left no memorial. To this, his own character contributed. Self-effacing he was not; but one might coin the expression "self-immersing." Athens as he made her was not only his life-work but his most abiding passion, loved to the detriment both of his property and of his family life. It was, indeed, perhaps his most tragic limitation that Greece, part from Athens, meant no more to him than Europe to most patriots of the present day; but few moderns can cast a stone at him there. His business was her business, his recreation the devising of new means of expression for Athenian art, song, athletics, and lyrical drama—that, and conversation with pioneer thinkers of his time on the physical or social sciences. His intimate friends included Sophocles, Pheidias, Anaxagoras the scientist, Damon the musician; the woman he loved was one whose intelligence was respected by Socrates. As a young man he was a soldier of conspicuous gallantry. He had also a dry, ironical humour, which appears not only in some of his few quoted sayings but in Thucydides' reports of a group of his last speeches—a humour which is certainly not Thucydides' own. Olympian to the outside world he may have been, but chilly—no. Even in Athens, no man lived more fully than Pericles.

If we know little of Pericles' early life, we do know chiefly from Herodotos, the "Father of History," a good deal about his family and background. His father was the admiral who crushed the remains of the Phœnician navy in the year after Salamis. His great-uncle founded the Athenian democracy. His great-great-great-grandfather bloodily crushed the first attempt to overthrow the old aristocracy, and bequeathed to his descendants a family curse that was still heard of in Pericles' time. The whole story of the rise of democracy in Athens is bound up with the history of that great family. For a candid historian, it is necessary in a biography of Pericles to use the word "probably" more often than one would wish. But no figure more clearly invites the attempt, in the terms of reference of this series, "by way of a biography of a great man to open up a significant historical theme."

PART I

ATHENS AND THE RISE OF PERICLES

Chapter 1

The Curse of the Alkmeonidai

PERICLES WAS BORN about 494 B.C., probably in the country house of his father, Xanthippos, at Cholargós, in the plain near Athens. He must have been over twenty in 473, when his name first appears in an extant official document; and he was still in full vigour—probably not over sixty-five—almost up to his death in 429. But no one has recorded the exact year of his birth; babies are seldom famous, even in the most distinguished families.

Certainly Pericles' family was distinguished. His father, Xanthippos, was a rising general and politician, and *his* father's name Ariphron, not a common name, also occurs in the list of Archons, or Regents, elected for life, centuries back, in the age when Athens had first reduced the old kingship to a purely religious office. Pericles had also a brother named Ariphron, no doubt an elder brother, since the eldest son usually bore his grandfather's name; and in having to play second fiddle to his brother, who was an entirely mediocre person, one may perhaps find that touch of repression in early childhood that is so common in the career of a successful man of action.

If Xanthippos' family was distinguished, that of Pericles' mother was famous throughout the Greek world. She came of the magnificent, brilliant, slightly sinister House of the Alkmeonidai, whose family history constituted no small part of the political history of Athens. They claimed descent from the family of the old King Nestor of the Trojan War, which had migrated to Athens when the wild Dorian conquerors overran the Peloponnese and founded the great military power of Sparta. Their family names, Alkmeon and Megakles, both appeared among the early Regents; and at the very beginning of Athenian history as recorded in any detail—perhaps in 632—a Megakles as Archon (by now a yearly office) defeated the attempt of a young noble named Kylon to subvert the ruling aristocracy and install himself as despot of Athens. Thereby hangs a tale: for Megakles also permitted or ordered the massacre of Kylon's followers, when they had left sanctuary on the promise of a fair trial, some of them even on holy ground; and thus originated the family curse, which was still in full operation two hundred years later, at least when political opponents found it convenient to rake it up.

Megakles had to go into exile, but his son Alkmeon was back by 590, perhaps under the amnesty arranged by the revered legislator Solon. He was a general in the crusade or Sacred War, waged by several Greek states against the port of Krissa, whose people had been charging unconscionable tolls on through-traffic to the sanctuary of Delphi. The episode was important in the family history; for while at Delphi, Alkmeon made some useful contacts. He was able to assist some envoys sent by the rich king of Lydia, in Asia Minor, to consult the oracle; and among the allied leaders he met Kleisthenes, the powerful despot of Sikyon, across the Corinthian Gulf, who later chose Alkmeon's son Megakles as husband for his only daughter Agariste. Runner-up in the competition for the lady's hand was another Athenian, Hippokleides son of Teisandros, of the house of the Philaïdai, who claimed descent from the hero Ajax, almost the only Athenian family to rival the Alkmeonidai in fame and prowess. He might, says Herodotos, even have won, had he not drunk too much on the last night of Kleisthenes' house-party for candidates, and danced upside down on a table in a manner unbefitting a gentleman. "So Megakles and Agariste were married," goes on Herodotos, "and to them were born Kleisthenes, who founded the Athenian democracy, and Hippokrates; and to Hippokrates, another Megakles and another Agariste, who, being married to Xanthippos the son of Ariphron and being with child, dreamed that she brought forth a lion; and after a few days, she brought forth Pericles to Xanthippos."

The political career of Megakles, the husband of the first Agariste, was chequered. He emerged as leader of the "Coast Party," based on the new class of merchants and ship-owners who had been given political importance under the Constitution of Solon (594); but the centre of the stage was stolen by another brilliant nobleman, Peisistratos, still farther to the "left," who by armed force made himself "tyrant" or uncrowned king of Athens, as leader of a "Highland party" of the poor peasants. Megakles for a time made alliance with Peisistratos against the conservative nobles, and gave him his daughter in marriage; but the marriage was childless—gossip said, by the intention of Peisistratos, who already had sons of his own; Megakles and Peisistratos quarrelled, and Megakles, like his grandfather, was finally driven into exile. In exile the Alkmeonidai renewed their connection with Delphi, taking the contract for the rebuilding of the great temple, which had been burnt down in 548; and it was from this point of vantage that Kleisthenes the son of Megakles intrigued against the sons of Peisistratos, finally inducing Sparta, by the influence of the powerful Oracle of Apollo, to eject Peisistratos' son Hippias about 510.

The descendants of Kleisthenes and of the nobles who were with him—they included an Alkibiades and an Andokides, both ancestors of namesakes famous in Pericles' time—took great credit to themselves as descendants of the liberators of Athens from "tyranny." In fact, Peisistratos, like many other "tyrants" of his age, was one of the greatest developers of his city's economic life, and by breaking the old aristocracy played an essential part in making possible the constitution that was to come. By Hippias' time, the work of the despotism was done, and commons as well as nobles saw the end of it without regret. The new and much more democratic constitution, which Kleisthenes then introduced and carried through the popular Assembly organised long ago by Solon, was indeed a notable piece of legislation, and gives Kleisthenes a place among the great men of a great age. But though the Alkmeonidai in exile had, it seems, learned some sympathy with classes outside the landed gentry of Attica, it would be a mistake to regard Kleisthenes' breadth of view as having anything to do with philanthropy. One of the most interesting documents discovered by the Ameri-

can excavators of central Athens, in fact, appears to be
a fragment of a list of Archons of the time of Hippias, inscribed on stone for public reference soon after the death
of Pericles:

(H)IPPIAS
(K)LEISTHEN(ES)
(M)ILTIADES
(?KA)LLIADE(S)
(?PEISI)STRAT(OS)

The letters in parentheses are broken away, and are con-
jectural.

Miltiades, who was head of the Philaïdai and later to
be famous as the victor of the Battle of Marathon, was
already recorded by an ancient historian as having been
archon in 524. Before him we have the names of Kleisthenes the Alkmeonid, 525, and Hippias himself—the
"Duce" taking his turn as official head of the republic—
in 526; while after Miltiades we have, probably, Kalliades
—a name known later in the immensely rich family of
the Hereditary Heralds of the great santuary of Eleusis—
and the younger Peisistratos, Hippias' son. With Kleisthenes, Miltiades, and Kalliades (if the Ka- is correct),
we find that members of all the three familes most prominent in Athens in the days of Pericles had not been above
accepting overtures from Hippias to serve under him, during a temporary "honeymoon, before plots and economic
difficulties made of Hippias a tyrant in the modern as well
as the ancient sense.

What happened after the expulsion of Hippias was at
first simply a recommencement of the old family rivalries
between the noble clans, until the astute Kleisthenes,
worsted in this game by a coalition of his rivals under
Isagoras the son of Teisandros (perhaps a Philaïd), in
Herodotos' words "enlisted the people in his party." The
famous constitution of Kleisthenes then followed. Kleisthenes might be no saint, but he was a great politician.
The people stuck to him through thick and thin, against
Isagoras and even against Sparta, when the Spartan king,

in dismay at what he had unleashed, tried to suppress the new constitution; and then, when the Spartan danger had passed, through the refusal of Sparta's allies to march to restore a tyranny, the Athenians turned against their northern enemies, the men of Chalkis and Thebes, got between them by a swift march, routed them both in two battles fought on one day, and actually captured the walled town of Chalkis, a feat almost unparalleled in Greek military history. This was the revolutionary war of the democracy of Athens; a war on which Herodotos, writing in the heyday of Pericles, comments: "From this one may see how noble a thing is political equality: the Athenians under a despotism were no better men in war than their neighbours, but when they were rid of it they proved far the best of them all. Hence it is clear that when they were under a master they made no effort, as men working for another; but when they were free, every man did his utmost in his own interest."

Fragments still remain from the inscription on the war memorial set up for this brilliant campaign—a war memorial which Pericles was, long after, to refurbish and rededicate, to cheer the spirits of Athens in a dark hour.

And yet not even Kleisthenes ended his days in peace and honour. He is said (by late writers) to have died in exile. The reason probably was his Persian policy.

While the little cities of Greece quarrelled over their miniature-scale local politics, that yet have so much significance for human history, the vast, well-organised empire of Persia, benevolent but despotic, had arisen in the east. Under the great Cyrus (Kurush), the new power engulfed Babylonia, Syria, Asia Minor and the Greek cities on its coast; under his successor, Egypt. Its king at this time was the very great idealist and administrator Daryavaush, Darius. Darius, like many of his nobles, believed that he had nothing less than a mission from God to organise and pacify the world. It was a great tragedy that this "new order" fell foul of the Greeks; the Greeks, chaotic and quarrelsome, but free and creative.

To Persia appealed the old Hippias, who, when Sparta failed to restore him, retired to an outpost on the Darda-

nelles, seized long since by his father, and was content to
rule it as a Persian vassal; and to it, in a fateful hour for
himself, appealed Kleisthenes, offering through ambassadors, in face of Sparta's support for reaction, to accept
Persian overlordship in the hope of saving his new insti-
tutions and his own position. By the time the ambassadors
returned, however, the danger had passed, thanks to
Sparta's allies and to the Athenians' own strong right arms;
and the people—showing, one much acknowledge, a surer
political instinct than Kleisthenes with all his brilliance—
turned in great anger against Kleisthenes and sought leaders of their own.

The Persian question dominated Greek politics throughout the childhood and youth of Pericles. When he was
born, the Greek cities of Ionia were in the last throes of
a grim, desperate, and mis-managed struggle to throw off
the Persian yoke. Athens supported the Ionians with a
contingent which distinguished itself by raiding Sardis, the
Persian capital of western Asia Minor; but after sustain-
ing a reverse in its retreat, the force was withdrawn—a
clear sign of divided counsels at home. There were still
supporters of the tyrants at large in Athens, for the democracy took no action against those who had personally
done no harm; and doubtless they urged that old Hippias
was the man best placed to reconcile to Persia an Athens
repentant of its late follies. In 496, after the reverse in
Ionia, they even carried the election of their leader, Hip-
parchos, as archon for the year. And on the dominant
issue of foreign policy at least, those experienced men of
the world, the leaders of the Alkmeonid faction, were disposed to agree with them.

Plain men, on the other hand, whether conservative
country squires or peasants or the city workmen (including many Asia Minor refugees, enfranchised by the legislation of Kleisthenes) were for making a fight of it. In
493 the archon elected was a portent: one Themistocles,
well-to-do—for the archon had to be a man of property
—but the son of an obscure *bourgeois* by a woman of
Asia Minor, for a hundred years the only man of the

people to become the acknowledged leader of democratic Athens.

In 490—probably the earliest historic event that Pericles could remember—came the inevitable Persian attempt to avenge Sardis and "take in" Athens. Hippias was with the invading fleet, and its leaders hoped for useful help from collaborators within the city. But they were disappointed. They were faced by an almost united people. Among the generals commanding the regiments of the ten new Tribes (artificial administrative divisions introduced by Kleisthenes), Themistocles served side by side with Aristeides the Just, an ex-supporter of Kleisthenes, and Miltiades the son of Kimon, the Philaïd chief. Miltiades, whose family under the tyrants had ruled over a Greco-Thracian kingdom of their own in the Gallipoli peninsula, was a picturesque, even formidable, figure. When he fled to Athens after the failure of the Ionian revolt, some of his enemies (who included the Alkmeonidai) had tried to get rid of him by prosecuting him as an ex-tyrant; but patriots saw in him first and foremost a good military expert, who was also well and truly compromised against Persia. The attack on him failed, and Miltiades survived to give the commander-in-chief Kallimachos invaluable advice, directly responsible for the great victory of Marathon.

Once the danger was passed, party strife broke out with renewed vigour; and this gives us the chief fact that is known about the early life of Pericles. Pericles was the first notable statesman to be brought up among leading parliamentarians in a democratic state—among, as one might say, the great Whig families, the Alkmeonidai and their allies.

On the morrow of Marathon, there were ugly rumours that the Alkmeonidai had been in league with the enemy. Somebody, certainly, had been heliographing with a bright shield from near Marathon Bay. But nothing could be proved, and Pericles' father felled the man who seemed the party's most dangerous rival, impeaching Miltiades for "deceiving the people"—which ranked as treason— after Miltiades had failed to liberate the Ægean islands that had submitted to Persia, in a campaign marked by unpopular and undemocratic secrecy. Miltiades was convicted, and only the memory of Marathon saved him from the death penalty. He died soon after from a wound which had gangrened, leaving his son Kimon, a youth of about nineteen, to pay a crippling fine of fifty talents— 300,000 drachmas, at a time when the silver drachma was the top wage paid per day to a skilled craftsman. Aristeides was elected archon for 489, and it seemed that the Alkmeonidai had consolidated their position. To Pericles, at the age of seven, in fact, the most interesting place in the world was probably the stables where his uncle Megakles kept the team of chariot horses that he was training for the next great four-yearly festival and race-meeting at Delphi.

Persia meanwhile was occupied with a rebellion in Egypt, and many men tried to forget the no longer imminent danger. But Themistocles did not forget. During the respite, which lasted for ten years, he worked steadily for two objects—an Athens purged of collaborators, and an increased navy, able to hold its own, at least in narrow waters, against the Phœnicians who fought for Persia.

The Athenian democratic constitution contained one highly original provision. With a view to the peaceful elimination of any future would-be Fuehrers, Kleisthenes is said to have laid down that at a fixed meeting of the Assembly every winter the people should vote on the question whether there was any citizen who should be removed. If the majority answered yes, a kind of election was held in the spring. Every citizen who chose wrote the name of his chief political bugbear on an *ostrakon*—a piece of broken pottery, "the waste paper of the ancient world" as it has been called—and, subject to a quorum of 6,000 voters, the recipient of the most votes went into honourable exile for ten years. The process was called "potsherding"—*ostrakismós*.

So far this weapon had not been used—which causes some scholars to doubt whether it was Kleisthenes' invention, as the tradition says, or more recent. In any case, it was Themistocles who brought it into use. In 487 Hip-parchos, the archon of 496 and leader of the Peisistratid party, was "ostracised." In the same year a law of great significance for the further democratisation of the state was passed. Henceforth, instead of electing annually an archon or regent, a king or religious head of the state, a commander-in-chief and six junior archons whose duties were chiefly judicial, the people would elect five hundred candidates—fifty from each of the ten tribes—and from these the nine archons and their secretary, one official from each tribe, would be chosen by lot. Naturally after this the archons rapidly lost prestige and influence; the "War Leader" in particular was at once a mere cipher in the hands of his ten generals, who were still directly elected. The main object at the time was probably that the chief executive positions might not be always in the hands of political leaders.

All this naturally went over the head of the child Pericles; but in 486 he was brought up against politics really sharply. His uncle Megakles was "potsherded," allegedly as being compromised on the side of the ex-tyrants. No doubt his friends remarked that the people were showing great ingratitude to the memory of Kleisthenes. Megakles himself did not take his fate tragically. He went off to Delphi, taking the horses with him. They won their chariot-race, and there still survives the little choral lyric which a young poet of Thebes—Pindar—wrote, for a suitable fee, to celebrate the occasion. Pindar had already written a very beautiful dirge for the funeral of old Hippokrates, Pericles' mother's father, of which some lines survive. The last great poet of the age of the nobles, which was now passing, was thus well known to the family of the future democratic leader.

When Pericles was nine, there was a sharper blow still. This time it was his own father who was to go. Xanthippos, it appears, had always kept clear of the ex-tyrant's friends; but he was a rival to Themistocles, and he was Megakles' brother-in-law. Last of all the leaders of Kleisthenes' old party went Aristeides, in 483, after a violent struggle over Themistocles' proposal to spend a large surplus, just realised from the state silver mines, on increas-

ing the navy. Even now—such is human nature—
Themistocles, in order to pass his navy bill, had to point
not to the distant and, as some thought, hypothetical danger from the east, but to the prospect of crushing a
parochial enemy: the island of Aigina, "the eyesore of
Piræus" as Pericles later called it, in full view from the
coast of Attica, which had an older tradition of sea-power
than Athens and, till then, a larger fleet.

With the help of this subterfuge the ships were ready,
just in time, before the great Persian invasion came in
480; and if many of the crews were still raw, the genius
of Themistocles made up for that.

The year 480 is Themistocles' year in history. It was
he who insisted on fighting as far forward as possible,
when most of the Peloponnesians, characteristically, were
in favour of defending only the Peloponnese. He held to
the original naval plan of holding the straits of Artemision, off a temple of Artemis at the north end of Euboia,
even when the land forces fell back from Thessaly, finding, like the British in 1941, that the Mount Olympos (or
Haliakmon) line is not nearly as strong as it sounds from
a distance. There the Greeks, with Themistocles' new
Athenian navy forming half their entire strength, inflicted
heavy loss on the enemy as they slipped, piecemeal for
lack of harbours on the coast of Thessaly, round the corner to their new base near modern Volo; while north-
easterly gales on that dangerous coast inflicted still greater
damage, including the loss of a whole enemy squadron
sent down the east coast of Euboia to cut the Greeks'
communications. This execution of Themistocles' plan
was made possible by the blocking of the coast road into
Greece at Thermopylæ, at the very last moment, by Leonidas, king of Sparta, acting apparently on his own initiative while the unwieldy allied war council at Corinth was
still arguing. Finally there was a gruelling fleet action off
Artemision, after which the Greeks were probably in no
state to renew the battle, even if the Persian "guard division," with a local guide, had not meanwhile made their
way over the mountains to cut off the gallant Leonidas;
but Themistocles in retreat was undismayed. He plied the

enemy's Ionian sailors with subversive propaganda; he nerved the Athenians to evacuate their country and city and to venture all on their fleet. He got the allied fleet, including useful reinforcements, sent to Salamis island, to help with the evacuation of Athens; and then tricked the Persians into rowing all night to cut off their retreat and attacking in the narrow straits at dawn. If ever a general changed the course of history for the better, Themistocles did so, in all that led up to the victory of Salamis. It is a thrilling story, but the place for its details is not here.

And yet, in spite of all, Themistocles was out of office in 479. What seems to have happened was that when Athens was evacuated and the Assembly could not be convened, the ancient and conservative council of ex-archons, called the Council of the Hill of Ares, or Areopagus, took charge of the administration, and settled appointments for the next year. Aristeides commanded the Athenian contingent in the army that routed the Persians in central Greece in 479, and Xanthippos that in the fleet, which destroyed the enemy remnants in the Ægean, and liberated Ionia. (All political exiles had been recalled in 480.) Aristeides, a year or two later, was entrusted by the liberated Ionian cities, as well as by Athens, with the organisation of a league of these cities for continued defence or aggression against Persia. The capital of the League was at the holy islet of Delos—a place chosen for its sanctity, and also (like Ottawa or Canberra) to avoid jealousy among the more important cities—but its executive, from the first, was Athenian. Both Xanthippos and Aristeides were thoroughly competent commanders, but it is noteworthy that Themistocles, though employed on some very important diplomatic missions to Sparta, was never again permitted to command the fleet which he had made.

Chapter 2

Education of a Radical

PERICLES, FOURTEEN YEARS OLD, must have boiled inwardly as he took part in the evacuation, with the women and children. He had probably just seen Kimon, the son of Miltiades, leading a group of young "knights" to dedicate their bridles to Athene on the Acropolis. It was a symbolic action; one dedicated to the gods things that one had finished with—one's toys on growing up, the tools of one's trade on retiring. Kimon was advertising his acceptance of Themistocles' thesis, that Athens' hope of safety was in her fleet. After hanging up his bridle and saying his prayers to the Goddess, Kimon took down from the temple wall an old infantry shield and went off to join his ship; to fight as a marine like any middle-class citizen, and to win commendation for valour in the Battle of Salamis. For the rest of his life, indeed, all Kimon's chief expeditions were to be sea-borne. But Pericles was not old enough; a hard fate for a high-spirited boy in such a crisis.

Many of the evacuees crossed the Gulf to Troizen, with which Athens had old ties of friendship. The little town received them nobly, even voting a grant from its own slender funds towards their maintenance and the schooling of the children. But many also, as well as the fighting men, went no farther than Salamis. Pericles' father, who had got home from exile in time to help with the evacuation, went there himself to join the forces and probably took his family. His favourite hound followed him and, when no animals could be allowed on board the densely crowded ships, plunged into the water and swam after them across the strait, only to die, exhausted, after dragging itself ashore. They buried it on a headland, and later set up a stone over its grave, which became a well-known landmark on the shore of Salamis.

Afterwards the Athenians came back, to a devastated land. The Persians had had special orders to deal severely with Athens, if she did not surrender, as a reprisal for the burning of Sardis during the Athenian offensive in Asia Minor. Every house had been systematically burnt except a few large ones, which had been used by high Persian officers. Even the temples stood roofless and fire-blackened, and the brightly painted marble statues of victorious athletes and girl acolytes lay shattered on the ground. The Athenians let them lie; they intended to make the enemy pay for the restoration of the temples; and meanwhile there was more immediate work to be done. Before they had got more than the most temporary roofs over their heads, the Athenians, rich and poor, men, women, and children, were at work on their new fortifications, while Themistocles went to Sparta and kept those already jealous "allies" in play with bland denials that anything was going on. Tombstones, sections of pillars, carved stones from the ruined monuments, all went into the walls; and when at last the Spartans, at Themistocles' suggestion, sent commissioners to see for themselves, they were quietly detained as hostages for the safe return of Themistocles and his colleagues.

There was also a religious service of thanksgiving for the great deliverance. The soloist was a very handsome boy from Kolonos, near Pericles' home, about the same age as Pericles, and for most of his life one of his closest friends. His name was Sophocles.

After these excitements were over there were still a few years for Pericles before the longed-for time when he could assume the duties and privileges of a grown-up citizen. Greek schooling was elementary only; one learned reading, writing, arithmetic, and music, and finished at about fourteen. In the next few years Athenian boys of well-to-do families amused themselves largely with athletics, at the gymnasia, running, wrestling, throwing the discus or javelin, and gossiping or discussing the world and its problems, while they lay about in the verandas or colonnades that served as dressing-rooms. They played a team game (with a small ball) which looks like basketball, and a game with a ball and curved sticks which looks like hockey, but may have been an individual game. Or they went hunting in the mountain forests, or got up club picnics down by the sea, to which each brought his contribution. There was much sowing of adolescent wild oats. But Pericles was a serious-minded boy, and one of those who were interested in finding out about the great world (much facilitated when one had such a father as Xanthippos) and about the novel and daring theories of the wise men of Ionia.

There were no sophists (free-lance popular lecturers) yet, such as there were thirty years later; but that did not prevent Ionian thought from reaching an *élite* at Athens. Young men in Pericles' day argued as their sons were to argue in the days of Socrates, and young men in Europe ever since. Forty years on, when Pericles' ward, Alkibiades, had successfully tried out Socrates' dialectic on his respected guardian, Pericles, verbally cornered, was constrained to laugh the matter off, like some millions of later fathers, guardians, and uncles, with an "Ah, my lad —I too was good at that sort of argument when I was your age."

Ionia, after its political and economic revolutions, had already been for a century in the full flush of an intellectual upheaval. Already in 585 b.c. Thales of Miletos, probably on the strength of the records kept for centuries by the priests of Babylon, predicted an eclipse of the sun. His pupil Anaximandros worked out views on the evolution of the earth, on geological change (observable in progress, in the rapid silting up of the mouth of the "Meander" river near Miletos) and therewith on the evolution of man, whom he believed, correctly, to be descended from a sea-beast. Xenophanes of the neighbouring Kolophon made observations on fossils, and mocked openly at the anthropomorphic gods. The Thracians' gods, he remarked, are blonde, and the negroes' gods negroid, and if oxen and horses could draw, no doubt they also would create their gods in their own image.

Greatest of all the Ionians was Herakleitos of Ephesos, known as The Obscure, a lonely genius, whose doctrine of the identity of opposites (foreshadowed by Anaximandros and almost forgotten after the time of Plato) was taken up (explicitly from Herakleitos) by Hegel. He is thus among the intellectual ancestors of Marx and Lenin; a fortune which would have surprised the aristocratic Herakleitos considerably. Herakleitos' doctrine was "All is flux; naught abides." "You cannot step into the same river twice." What prevents this ever-becoming world from being a chaos is Measure. (In this Herakleitos is thoroughly Greek.) The world is a "harmony [meaning also 'a structure'] of opposite tensions, as in the lyre and the bow." All things are relative; everything is more or less its opposite—"the way up and the way down are the same"; "good and bad are the same thing." Our conventional judgments are the result of a partial vision: "To God, all things are beautiful and good and just; but men suppose some things to be just and some unjust." Herakleitos' God is (like Xenophanes') an indwelling spirit, immanent in the world, but not its creator, the world having existed "always"; but as no word for "spirit" had yet been evolved, what he says is that "It is a fire." Elsewhere he adds: "That which alone is wise both wishes and does not wish to be called Zeus"; i.e. this "wise" fire is in a way personal, but not to be confused with the black-bearded polygamist of the mythology. Fire, too, are the spirits of men; and fire is matter—matter in its most refined and active form, which is convertible into the ordinary gaseous, liquid, and solid forms (air, water, earth) in a species of "commerce." Herakleitos compares the unthinking multitude to men asleep: for "men awake have one public world; but men asleep turn aside, each into a private world of his own."

It was all very exciting. The doctrines of the physicists were soon being discussed in every market-place, in the street, at parties, and on shipboard. Over in Sicily they were already being very charmingly parodied by the playwright Epicharmos. One of Epicharmos' characters argued, for example, that as we are different to-day from what we were yesterday, we cannot reasonably be sued to-day for yesterday's debts.

A little later, probably, than these years of his adolescence, Pericles fell in with an Ionian ideally qualified to satisfy his desire for enlightenment. From Ionia to Athens (just when is uncertain[1]) came one Anaxagoras of Klazomenai, a man not many years older than Pericles himself. He came of a land-owning family, but in his passion for philosophy had neglected his property and let his estate sink to the condition of rough pasture. Such an otherworldly intellectual was no person to fend for himself in the anxious, embittered, post-war world of newly liberated Ionia. One would like to think that Pericles himself invited him to Athens; he certainly maintained him when there.

The possibilities of Ionian materialism were getting worked out by this time, and Anaxagoras postulated at the beginning of things an intervention of Mind, which "separated and arranged" things, hitherto mingled together in the primeval chaos. "Mind," however, performed no further function in his scheme of things which thenceforth ran on purely mechanical principles—a feature which was to disappoint the religious-minded sceptic, Socrates. Perhaps, as Cornford suggests, Anaxagoras considered his intervention of Mind a "minimum postulate."

Anaxagoras believed in a plurality of worlds, since worlds (including men and women and civilisations) have probably emerged under similar circumstances at various

[1] His life by the late Greek hack-writer, Diogenes Laertios, says that Anaxagoras was born in 500 B.C., and "began to philosophise at the age of twenty, at Athens, in the Archonship of Kallias" (i.e. Kalliades, 480 B.C.). This statement, which some modern scholars strangely try to accept, is—one would have thought it was obvious —a misunderstanding by the good Diogenes of his sources, which presumably said "at the age of twenty, in the Archonship of K. at Athens"—the archonship being simply mentioned as a standard way of giving the date. Athens in the year of Xerxes' invasion was scarcely the place to which a young man intent on studying philosophy would migrate; and, moreover, Anaxagoras' neglect of his property (which is mentioned by Plato) was presumably in adult life rather than in his 'teens.

times and places within the Infinite. In his doctrine of matter he borrowed something from Herakleitos' "unity of opposites." There are atoms, he held, corresponding to every form of matter existing in the world; but no matter is completely pure; even "snow is black." His chief glory is that he was the first to form a correct notion of the nature of the sun and moon—prompted perhaps by his observations on a huge meteorite which fell in the Gallipoli Peninsula in 462—and thence to give the true account of the causes of eclipses.

Pericles found Anaxagoras' conversation immensely stimulating. Anaxagoras became a well-known if somewhat shocking figure in religious and intellectually conservative Athens, and was nicknamed Nous, after the "Mind" in his working hypothesis. It was from him, in Plato's estimation, that Pericles derived that philosophic elevation of mind and scientific approach that distinguished his oratory and outlook from those of any other politician of his day.

No Plato has recorded the conversations of young Pericles and young Sophocles and their friends in those years after the Persian War. But even so we can know something, and infer more, about that circle of friends and acquaintances, and the intellectual climate of the years in which Pericles grew to manhood.

As the son of the great Xanthippos by a daughter of the Alkmeonidai, Pericles naturally knew "everybody" in Athenian society, and was early known himself as a brilliant young man who, if he lived, would make his mark. People certainly began asking when he was going to start speaking in the Assembly when he was nearer twenty than thirty. Among older men who were later his political associates were Kleinias, whose father Alkibiades had been with Kleisthenes in the revolutionary wars, gallant and debonair, very much the soldier, and Kallias, hereditary Torch-bearer of the Mysteries and the richest man in Athens. Kallias was also rudely known as "Money-in-the-Hole," from a scandalous story that he had been shown some treasure by a Persian who surrendered to him at Marathon, and had buried the money and killed his prisoner to prevent him telling anyone else. Others who knew the young Pericles well included the impressive figure of Æschylus, fine soldier, poet and thinker, and Kimon the son of Miltiades, who had served under Xanthippos, and himself became Athens' leading general before he was thirty-five.

Among friends of Pericles' own age the best-known name is that of Sophocles. They were neighbours, they were nearly the same age, both were well-born, well-to-do, and in mind brilliant, serious, and idealistic. Sophocles, no doubt, was more interested in poetry, Pericles in war and politics; Sophocles was religious, Pericles a rationalist, interested in Ionian science; Sophocles was passionate and amorous, Pericles, for a Greek of his age, almost austere. But there was no division yet in Athens between men of action and æsthetes. Civilisation was still integrated. Pericles, like every intelligent man, was interested as a matter of course in the art and poetry which expressed the spirit of Athens; and Sophocles the poet, like every good citizen, was a man of action too. Long afterwards, in the year in which he produced his *Antigone,* he and Pericles were generals together.

The strongest influence on Pericles' intellectual development in youth is said to have been that of his music-teacher, one Damon or Damonides.

Music was felt by the Greeks to be an art that every educated man should practise, and the theory of music to be a study appropriate to philosophers—one of the possible approaches to the heart of things. In the previous generation Pythagoras, having discovered that not only the shapes of triangles but the notes of the lyre depended upon certain mathematical proportions, had erected on this basis a whole philosophy, an extraordinary blend of mysticism and mathematics, which deeply influenced later Greek thought. Damon's was the converse development. He was not a philosopher with an interest in music, but a musician with a bent for philosophy and politics. He seems not to have belonged to the circle of the great political families; and, in fact, he was probably the young Pericles' most intimate contact with the world outside that circle. Not many years older than his pupil, he remained his friend through life. He gets a bad "Press" from the later conservative pamphleteers and gossiping historians; for it was said to have been under his influence that Pericles, the most brilliant Athenian noble of his day, entered politics as a radical.

We have seen what Herodotos, writing during the Periclean Age, said about democracy (or "the equal voice" in politics) as a tonic to the morale of a people. Already in his youth Pericles' democratic idealism was forming, and with it a devoted patriotism towards the city that was the bearer of this ideal; a patriotism that was something new in history; in a phrase of his old age, nothing less than passionate love towards the city of Athens.

For the rest, the spirit of the age at Athens was—like Pericles himself—serious, intent and, in comparison with previous generations, austere. Even dress was being simplified, as often under a rising democracy—for the new politically important class regards the luxury of the old one with a mixture of envy and contempt. Only the older rich men now wore the long, soft Ionian tunic, hanging to the ankles, and used gold "grasshopper" brooches to fasten up their long hair. The new fashions, both for men and women, were simpler; for women the Dorian (or as we say "classic") *peplos,* whose beauty depended on its draping, not on embroidery and innumerable pleats; for men, the Dorian tunic to the knees, with the *himation,* a simple rectangular woollen plaid, draped over it. Both fashions were borrowed from Sparta, which though under a military, authoritarian régime had established a rule of social equality between all full citizens. In literature, the last great masters of the aristocratic lyric poetry, Simonides and Pindar, were still active, but they had no successors; it was Æschylus, father of the new poetry of the theatre, whom the young Sophocles meant to emulate. But it is in art that one can see most clearly the new austerity.

The most noticeable change in sculpture is the disappearance of the "archaic smile," the naïve, automatic, "party smile" of past generations. In the new age, even the statues of victorious athletes show the new seriousness. It is one of them, a work of these very years of Pericles' adolescence—a fair-haired head found on the Acropolis, with traces of the painting of hair and eyes still undestroyed—that J. D. Beazley has hailed as "the first of that long and wonderful line of fifth-century boy-victors, not elated in the hour of their triumph, but grave and even troubled, as if made conscious, for the first time, of the meaning of life."

To say that the spirit of the time was serious and earnest is not, of course, to say that it was melancholy. All indications are that it was a happy, because a confident, age, an age in which every normal Athenian, landed nobleman or *bourgeois* democrat, craftsman, poet, or farmer, had a clear idea of what he wanted to do, and high hopes of doing it.

The artists, in addition to abolishing the archaic smile, were working towards a truer and less conventional portrayal of the human form; in a word, towards greater realism. Beazley says, again, of a typical athlete-statue of the new school: "The weight is no longer equally distributed between the two legs, but rests principally on one, here the left; the left hip is consequently higher than the right, the shoulders are uneven, the spine curves, the axis of the whole body is thrown out, and the head turns to one side instead of looking straight in front of it."

One would like to know if some of the old gentlemen with gold grasshoppers in their hair did not sometimes describe the new sculptures in very much these terms, and comment "Disgusting!"

Politically, as often after a war, it was a time of reaction. The Council of Areopagus, like the Roman Senate in the war with Hannibal, having distinguished itself in a crisis, showed every sign of trying to perpetuate its political leadership. Composed as it still was chiefly of men *elected,* before 487, to the highest offices of state, it concentrated in its ranks the best political experience of Athens, and it had ancient traditional though not statutory powers through which it could, if united, almost control the working of the constitution; especially that of arraigning as an offender against law or public decency anyone of whose conduct the Areopagites disapproved. The conservative majority of Areopagites at this time were united. Their leaders, to whom Themistocles had played cuckoo in the nest in the years between the wars, adopted his big-navy policy, but drew together against him personally. Themistocles found himself in opposition and losing ground. Jealousy against him probably played a large part. He was believed to have enriched himself enormously during his political career, and his reported sayings breathe a complacency that was tactless, even if justified. One of his acts, which did him no good in the long run, was to dedicate a temple to Artemis the Best in Counsel, in memory of his own achievements. Another— at least interesting—was in 476 to pay for the production, at the spring dramatic festival, of a tragedy (at this time a kind of oratorio), not on one of the usual, traditional, mythological themes, but on the Battle of Salamis.

The poet was a veteran, one Phrynichos. Eighteen years before, at the time of Themistocles' archonship, he had produced a similar historical piece called *The Fall of Miletos,* representing the ruin of Ionia in such heart-rending terms that the Athenians, with a bad conscience about their withdrawal of support, fined the poet, probably on the pretext of "impiety" (mixing the religious and the mundane).

No such bitterness marred the present occasion. Phrynichos won the prize for tragedy, and lyrics from the play were still popular fifty years later. It was too late to save Themistocles; but among those who applauded most warmly *The Phœnician Women* (the chorus represented wives of the defeated sailors) were Æschylus, a slightly younger veteran, and the young Pericles.

One wonders whether relations were strained between old Xanthippos and his intellectual-radical son; for Pericles made no secret of the fact that he admired Themistocles. But probably before 473, too soon to see the exile of his old enemy, Xanthippos died.

Pericles found himself a fairly rich man; and he at once proclaimed his political sympathies by paying— probably volunteering to pay, out of turn—for the plays entered by Æschylus at the festival of 472. Among the four plays, which made up a poet's regular entry, one still survives: *The Persians,* a play in which Æschylus rehandled to his own satisfaction the subject of *The Phœnician Women,* and the only surviving example of these early Athenian experiments in dramatising the history of their own times. It was one of Æschylus' greatest successes; and thus, appropriately, the name of Pericles made its first appearance in Athenian history.

But in spite of all efforts, Themistocles lost his battle with the Areopagus. Probably in 472 he himself was ostracised. He lived for some years at Argos, during which period democracy on the Kleisthenic model made rapid strides there and elsewhere in the Peloponnese, to Sparta's alarm. Then Sparta claimed to have evidence that he was in communication with Persia. He was impeached at Athens, in absence, by one Leobotes, son of Alkmeon (significant name!) and found guilty. Argos could no longer shelter him; and after an adventurous escape, up the west coast of Greece, across the wild Pindos mountains, across the Ægean, passing through an Athenian fleet under an assumed name, Themistocles lived out his remaining years as a pensioner of the Persian king.

Chapter 3

Pericles and Kimon

HIS OWN and Æschylus' victory with *The Persians* made
Pericles a public figure. His name had been brought before the public on a public occasion, and the suggestion
was already made to him that he should begin to speak
in the Assembly. His family's prestige would be an acqui-
sition to the radicals, and his intellectual brilliance was
fully appreciated.

Pericles very wisely put the suggestion aside as premature. For a young man of his age, however distinguished, to put himself forward in this way would have
been unpopular with many, and would have given a
handle to the conservatives. His reported excuse, that he
"had no desire to be ostracised," was probably a joke;
ostrakismós was a danger to leaders rather than to young
politicians. But Pericles felt that he had become quite
conspicuous enough. Already old men who remembered
Peisistratos (they must have been very old men, for
Peisistratos had been dead for nearly sixty years) were
saying that in face and voice Pericles strangely resembled
him.

Politics must wait for the present. In the meantime
Pericles threw himself into the task of winning a good
name by his conduct as a soldier.

There could not have been a more exhilarating time for
such an enterprise. As the acknowledged leaders of the
liberated cities organised in the Delian League, the
Athenians sent their fleets abroad year by year, reducing
the Persian garrisons that still held on grimly in Europe,
cleaning up pirates' nests like that of the fierce islanders
of Skyros, liberating towns on the long peninsulas of Asia
Minor where pro-Persian tyrants still held out with their
mercenaries; working in every way to secure the Ægean

against a Persian *revanche,* which was fully expected. The fighting was seldom desperate, and uniformly successful. The name of Athens had never stood so high.

The chosen general of Athens was Kimon, who had served under Xanthippos years ago when they were breaking the Persian hold on the Dardanelles. Kimon was on the crest of the wave at this time. After the condemnation of his father he had been, for a time, so crushed with debt that he could not even raise a dowry for his half-sister Elpinike. Consequently, in accordance with Greek custom, he could not himself marry; so Elpinike stayed at home and kept house for her brother, giving rise to scandalous stories in the normal course of gossip. Kimon had avoided selling the family lands, though sales of land were quite legal; but he was so beset with mortgages that he had seldom two silver pieces to rub together. From this position he was rescued by Kallias the Rich, a long-sighted politician, who for love of Elpinike—and no doubt also seeing that Kimon might be a most valuable connection—married her undowered and also paid off the debt outstanding for Miltiades' fine. Handsome, dashing, and popular, Kimon was also perhaps the best general ever produced by Athens. Knowing the general well no doubt also contributed still further to making these years for Pericles among the happiest in a life that knew much happiness; these summers when he idled on the fore-deck talking with other young volunteer marines, while the rowers and sails sent the triremes at six knots over the rippling blue Ægean; or panted in his heavy armour through the shallows and up beaches against enemies who always broke before the dreaded Athenians; or landed for the night at the little island harbours and sampled the island wine. As the old song had it:

> *"To mortal man, first gift is Health;*
> *The next is Beauty; third is Wealth—*
> *Wealth that no shame attends;*
> *The fourth is to be young among your friends."*

There were other things that people added to the list in Pericles' circle: to be well-thought-of in one's city, and that one's city itself should be prospering. Pericles had all these things.

Pericles had time also to see the first rising shadow of certain problems that were to become crucial for the Delian League.

The trouble was that the keen, efficient Athenians, who had become inured to business-like habits during the training of the new navy and the great war itself, found the Ionians and islanders chronically slow and unmilitary. To the island farmers, fishermen, and small traders, it seemed to matter very little if a contingent was a ship or two short of its quota or arrived a little late at its rendezvous. If one was not quite ready on the day appointed, was not tomorrow also a day? But the Athenians took their stand on the covenant of the League. If a contingent was not duly forthcoming, their generals would send a trireme to find out why, and to demand the balance in money to make up the agreed quota according to the Assessment of Aristeides. The allies resented these exactions and this insistence on punctuality, and found the Athenians' undisguised consciousness of superior efficiency none the more welcome from the fact that it was justified. Moreover, as the years passed and the apparent imminence of the Persian danger receded, compulsory naval service became increasingly unpopular, and the question whether another campaign this year was really necessary was increasingly asked. The intermittent friction which is, alas, almost a normal feature of relations between allies, became exacerbated until throughout the Ægean the Athenians, though still admired, were generally unpopular. The enthusiasm of the early days waned rapidly.

It was Kimon himself who pointed out a more excellent way. Allies who found it troublesome to produce their contingents regularly should be permitted and even encouraged to compound for the appropriate sum in money, paying it into the central treasury of the League at Delos. With this money Athens herself would supply additional ships; and allied sailors, if good enough, could serve aboard them for pay, alongside the men of Athens herself. Many of the small states whose contingent for a fleet of two hundred sail would be a fraction of a trireme (i.e. who would have to produce one ship jointly or in rotation with neighbours) compounded at once, and for a time everyone was satisfied. The Athenians were able to maintain an increased navy out of the allies' contributions; adventurous young men, who were glad to serve, could do so; the efficiency of the League fleets was greatly increased, and the presidents and councillors of the petty townships returned to parish-pump politics with a sigh of relief. Soon only a few of the larger and more efficient contingents were still provided by allied states direct.

Kimon was a brilliant soldier without political ideas except for a genial conservatism in what might well seem to him the best of all possible worlds; and it is very unlikely that he foresaw the consequences to which his policy would lead.

When Pericles was about twenty-five, the League was faced with its first major crisis. Naxos, the largest island of the Cyclades, which had once successfully stood a siege by the Persians and ruled an "empire" among the surrounding islets, declined to produce either ships or money; and when the Athenians sent to demand them the Naxians shut the gates in their faces and announced their withdrawal from the League.

Legally, the Naxians were in the wrong. To decide on any given campaign may have lain with the League conference at Delos, or with the Athenians alone, as leaders; but certainly it did not lie with individual states to decide whether to serve. The Covenant of the League envisaged war with Persia as a normal state of affairs, at least as long as Persia claimed overlordship over any Greek cities; and the Persian king had not yet abated any of his claims. It was indeed only commitments elsewhere in his vast empire that had prevented him from making any serious military effort in the west since 479, in which year the withdrawal of Xerxes and a great part of his field army had been caused not by the naval defeat at Salamis but chiefly by the revolt of Babylon. As for withdrawing from the League, the original members (of whom Naxos was one) had solemnised their treaty by sinking lumps of iron in the sea and swearing solemn alliance "till the iron should float." The Athenians did not hesitate. They block-aded Naxos and starved it into surrender. Naxos was dis-qualified from possessing warships, and was sentenced to pay her annual quota in money.

There seem to have been other similar withdrawals by minor members perhaps in the hope that the Athenians would not trouble to coerce them. But the Athenians did trouble. Whatever the legal position, there was some shak-ing of heads among conservatives at Athens over this coercion of free Greek republics; it was at least repugnant to Greek political ideals. But probably fewer Athenians doubted the step at the time than in after years.

Pericles was not among the doubters. To him it was clear that there had never been a city like Athens, and that Athens' right, destiny, and duty was to lead others. Athens had much to teach the Greek world; had not Argos, where Themistocles had resided in exile, already imitated every feature of the Athenian democracy? And meanwhile it was a first duty to smite the Persian.

Probably in the following year, a League fleet of two hundred sail under Kimon—heavy galleys carrying no less than forty armoured marines apiece on deck—assembled at Knidos, in the south-east Ægean, and sailed for the Levant. Phaselis, a rich Greek commercial city on the south coast of Asia Minor, held by Persia and stood a siege, but submitted before long, after mediation by the men of Chios, who were old commercial associates. Pha-selis paid ten talents down and a quota of six per annum thereafter.

The fleet sailed on eastward. Kimon had intelligence of a Persian fleet concentrating at the River Eurymedon, whether for defence or for renewed aggression (as some believed) is not clear. Probably it was mobilised only in answer to the Greek threat; for in spite of the delay at Pha-selis, Kimon's advance caught it before all its squadrons were in. Eighty ships from the Phœnician cities in Cyprus had not arrived, and without them the Persian commander Ariomandes was not anxious to fight; but he tried to defend his forward base at the Eurymedon. His ships lined up across the wide river mouth; but his Phœnician and Cilician sailors had no heart for the battle. When the Greeks with magnificent *élan* swept in to attack they gave way at once, and fled for refuge to their stockaded lines, held by Persian troops, on shore. It was a vain hope; for the Athenians and Ionians followed them up, grounded their triremes in the shallows, poured up the beach in a roaring, cheering wave, stormed across ditches and palisades and captured the camp too, despite brave resistance by the Persians. It was a total and complete destruction, and Kimon followed it up by putting to sea again, with men on his leading galleys dressed in Persian uniforms, and catching and destroying the eighty ships from Cyprus with nearly all their crews. It was the greatest and proudest achievement of the Delian League.

Between campaigns Greek armies always went home for the winter, except in the case of sieges, for which Athenian armies were becoming famous; so Pericles had no lack of opportunity to see his friends and keep his finger on political pulses. It is said to have been as early as 469 that his voice, with those "overtones" that reminded the old men of Peisistratos, was first heard in the Assembly.

The advanced democrats, on whose side he spoke, were still in a minority; though their leader Ephialtes, a man poor but incorruptible, was working hard to restore their fortunes. Year after year, when generals or archons gave account of their actions, according to the law of Solon, Ephialtes took the lead in asking awkward questions and in pressing for a condemnation if he deemed it just. Other men might be persuaded, for a consideration, to suppress charges or not press them too hard; but not Ephialtes. His was indeed a role which came to be expected of an Athenian popular leader; a useful and even necessary function in the commonwealth, but not one likely to be popular in influential circles. Ephialtes already had several convictions to his name, especially of archons. The well-to-do mediocrities, who staffed these offices under the system of drawing lots among five hundred candidates, were by no means always proof against the temptations attaching to their still important positions. The survivors, entrenched in the Council of Areopagus, hated Ephialtes bitterly.

The conservatives' greatest asset was the prestige and popularity of Kimon. Of princely wealth, now that his family estates were unencumbered, and richer still from personal spoils of war and from the presents showered upon even the most uncorrupt general abroad, Kimon was also debonair, approachable, generous, and open-handed. He kept open house to all members of his ward of Lakiadai; his orchards and vineyards were unfenced, that passers-by might help themselves. With his own wealth and the sums which he paid into the Treasury from spoils of war—in whose disposal his voice naturally carried weight with the Assembly—he and his contemporaries began that beautification of Athens which Pericles was to continue. Peisianax, a connection of the Alkmeonidai, built what was later known as the Painted Colonnade, which became the seat of judgment of the "King"; Leagros the Handsome restored the Altar of the Twelve Gods in the market-place; the Council House was rebuilt; the south wall of the Acropolis was completed; and Kimon planted plane-trees round the market-place, and laid out the shady and well-watered park at the Grove of Akademos, where Plato was to teach his friends, a hundred years later.

Ephialtes' aim above all was to deprive the irresponsible Areopagus—irresponsible in that its members held office for life—of those far-reaching judicial functions for which, except in cases of homicide, there was no statutory sanction. Until the people itself resumed these lost functions (so he would have put it), there could never be a real people's state in the sense in which Themistocles had understood it. The end was not yet, but his prosecutions of ex-archons were paving the way. Certainly, things were moving.

One sign of the times was in the field of poetry. Æschylus, in 468, lost the prize for tragedy to the twenty-seven-year-old Sophocles. There was great excitement over the decision; in fact, the judges are said to have committed their functions, *honoris causa,* into the hands of Kimon and the other generals, home triumphant, perhaps from the siege of Naxos.

The natural sequel to the Eurymedon would have been a campaign to liberate Greek Cyprus; but it was not to be. In 465 there was again trouble in the Ægean; this time in the north. Athens was projecting a colony at Nine Ways, on the Strymon above Eion in the gold-mining country. This brought her into conflict with the formidable neighbouring Thracians, with Macedonia (still a half-civilised and unstable feudal kingdom), and with the Greeks of Thasos, a powerful island state, who had long exploited gold deposits and trade with the natives, at great profit to themselves. Thasos withdrew from the League and prepared for resistance.

This was war in earnest. Thasos was a more serious opponent than Naxos, and even attempted naval operations—probably to attack the great convoy bringing up troops against the island. But Kimon with the covering fleet swept the Thasians from the sea with the loss of thirty-three galleys, and the landing was effected. The Thasians sent off a secret appeal to Sparta as the old leader of Greece, begging her to save Thasos and put an end to Athenian aggression by attacking Attica herself.

Kimon drew his blockading lines round Thasos town, and at the same time no less than ten thousand Athenian and League colonists under Leagros descended upon Nine Ways and made preparations to settle there. There seem also to have been successful operations against Macedonia, and some of the troops indulged in wild dreams of conquering the whole country; but Kimon, to their disgust and bewilderment, broke off the campaign. He may have had news from farther east that gave him pause; for the colony at Nine Ways met with disaster. Leagros, trying to strike a decisive blow at the Thracians, who were harassing the place, pushed imprudently inland; he was waylaid by a horde of barbarians (a coalition of the tribes), and he himself with the greater part of his force was cut to pieces.

But all this did not help Thasos. Sparta, already jealous of Athens, was willing to help and secretly promised to do so; but before she had made any overt move she was visited by disaster. An earthquake demolished almost every house in the town; there was tremendous loss of life, and immediately the flame of a serf revolt (perhaps already going on on a guerilla scale in the mountains) spread from end to end of her territories.

Thasos held out through two winters, against increasing hunger, but no help came, nor any weakening of the Athenian blockade. In 463 she surrendered; her fleet was confiscated, her walls were breached, and she was sentenced to pay an indemnity, and tribute in lieu of ships in future.

About this time—a notable political portent—Ephialtes and probably Pericles, the latter at almost the minimum legal age, were elected generals; for it was probably during the siege of Thasos, or soon after, that Pericles with fifty ships, and in another year Ephialtes with so few as thirty, carried out sweeps in the Levant—reconnoitring, and showing Persia that Athens still had ships to spare. Such liberties could be taken since the Eurymedon.

Ephialtes also decided that the time had come for a full-scale political battle, in the form of an attack on Kimon.

Kimon came home from Thasos to find the Assembly in a difficult temper. He had dealt with the revolt, but the disaster in Thrace and withdrawal from Macedonia meant failure on the wider issue. The democrats impeached him on the charge of accepting bribes from King Alexander of Macedon, and called upon Pericles (who no doubt had served in the campaign) to take part in the attack. Unwillingly enough, Pericles prepared to assail his old friend and general.

While the case was pending, Pericles was told that there was a woman at his door wishing to speak with him. Surprised—for he was well know as a *sérieux*—he bade his servants admit her. Unveiling her face—for she was doing a most unladylike thing by all Greek standards in calling on a man—the woman stood revealed as the now middle-aged Elpinike, come to plead with Pericles on behalf of her brother.

Pericles said: "Aren't you rather old, Elpinike, for adventures like this?"

He refused to make any rash promises. Nevertheless, when the trial came on, he refrained from any of the personal abuse that was common form in Greek law courts, and spoke strictly to his brief, quietly, straightforwardly, giving the facts as he knew them. Kimon for his part laughed at the charge. Could he not, he asked, have been *Proxenos* (official representative at Athens) of many rich Ionian or Thessalian states, who would pay well for his services? Yet he refused them, and did this service only for the sober Spartans who used no money. Was he likely to take bribes, then? Kimon was acquitted.

Soon afterwards there was another trial of strength. Sparta was faring so ill in her Helot war that at last she put her pride in her pocket and appealed for help to her allies—including Athens, under the treaty dating from the Great Persian War. There was a fierce debate. The democrats, though they knew nothing yet of Sparta's secret promise to Thasos, were against helping this stronghold of oligarchy; but Kimon carried the day with a passionate plea for Sparta, which he idealised. "Will you," he ended, "stand by and see Greece lamed of a leg, and Athens drawing the plough without her yokemate?"

Four thousand armoured men, a full third of Athens' field-army, under Kimon himself, marched to help Sparta. But the result was unexpected. The Spartans, "growing afraid of the Athenians' daring and revolutionary spirit," says Thucydides, "and fearing that they might be won over by the enemy, sent them away, the only allies to be so treated, without cause rendered, but simply saying that they did not require them further."

Some of the Atherian infantry, we must suppose—for the Spartans might be stupid but they were not lunatics —had been expressing themselves freely about the social and political conditions that they had found. They had been told they were going to suppress a slave-revolt; they found themselves opposed to good Greeks fighting against oppression—like the Athenians' own fathers.

This failure of Spartan diplomacy tipped the scale at Athens against Sparta's friends. Furious, the Assembly denounced the alliance with Sparta, and made new ones with Argos and Thessaly, states that had not been on the nationalist side in the Persian War. Almost at the same time (462-461), Ephialtes and Pericles carried their bill depriving the Areopagus of all powers except those of a supreme court for charges of murder. Its customary jurisdiction in moral and constitutional questions went, respectively, to the popular jury-courts and to the Council of Five Hundred—both, in effect, committees of the Sovereign People in Parliament Assembled.

Kimon, who appears to have been absent when the Areopagus bill was passed, flung himself into the fray on his return and tried to get it repealed. He failed. Political passions rose to fever heat, and resort was had to *ostrakismós,* as in the days of Themistocles. Kimon lost, and was sent into exile for ten years.

Ephialtes was now the leading citizen of Athens; but he did not long survive. Probably in the same year he was assassinated by a Boiotian bravo, in the pay—few people had any doubt—of a reactionary Athenian secret society.

So Kimon's ideal of a Greece united under the joint leadership of Athens and Sparta failed, as it was bound to fail. Democracy and the "national socialism" of Sparta were too ill-matched ever to be the "yoke-fellows" of the naïve, honest general's dream. Henceforth the alternatives were clearly posed: Athens *or* Sparta. It remained to be seen what the growing, teeming democracy could make of the new situation.

Chapter 4

A General of the Republic

A MODERN reader easily slips into thinking of the crisis of 462-461 B.C. in terms of modern democratic government, as though Kimon were a prime minister defeated in a general election and succeeded by Ephialtes and Pericles. This tendency is encouraged by the way in which later Greek writers make Kimon responsible for every feature of Athenian policy until his exile, and Pericles after it; a view followed, naturally but incautiously, by some moderns. One has to remind one's self again that *there was no Athenian prose literature* before the last years of Pericles' life, so that the tradition which we have of him is almost entirely a tradition of Pericles as the great political leader. Partly as a result, the historians of the next century early began to dramatise fifth-century politics by making Pericles responsible for the whole movement in which he played a part. Pericles made peace with Persia (but not till 449!) and led Athens into imperialism, war with Greeks, and defeat, ran the argument; while Kimon, as a foil, was written up as the good conservative, identified with the war with Persia, friendship with Sparta, and the leadership of free and willing allies. If one ignores generalisations and keeps one's eyes on what actually was done, one is at once struck by the facts that the first attempted secessions from the League took place in Kimon's time and that the war with Persia continued as energetically as ever for years after his exile.

This brings us to a second, a modern misconception, which arises from equating Pericles' position with that of a modern prime minister or American president.

The difference lies between the "direct democracy" of the Athenian city-state and representative democracy, which an Athenian would not have considered a democracy at all. Athens did not elect a parliament or president

61

or a government of any kind. It elected or chose by lot sundry committees and officials, some of them very important; but in addition to calling them to account at the end of their year, the Sovereign People itself directed them on all major issues, at meetings of the Assembly held at least four times in every five weeks, in addition to special meetings as required. The whole body of citizens, or such as chose to attend—great and small landed proprietors, merchants, shopkeepers, employers of labour, and an increasing majority of plain manual workers—formed at once the Athenian legislature and the supreme deliberative and policy-making body. The Athenian people did not choose but *was* its own government.

The people—Demos, later personified and put on the stage by Aristophanes as a peppery, goodhearted, short-sighted, John-Bullish old householder, liable to be hood-winked by a plausible steward—conducted its routine business through an array of committees and boards of annually changing officials; not permanent career-officials, but ordinary citizens giving up their time to the service of the state. It is time to give some account of the structure of that democracy, in which Pericles for the rest of his life played a leading role.

Chief pivot of the whole machinery was the Council; not the Areopagus, now deprived of political importance, but the Council of Five Hundred, commonly known as The Council, *par excellence*. First constituted of four hundred members by Solon, it consisted, since Kleisthenes, of fifty members from each of Kleisthenes' ten tribes, selected annually by lot from all citizens over thirty who volunteered. There seems to have been no lack of volunteers, and to make recruitment easier it was permitted to citizens to serve in the Council twice; but not more often, and not in successive years. The Council's chief function was to prepare business for the Assembly, and one of the few rules of procedure which the Assembly strictly observed was that no business whatever was to come before it which had not been before the Council. Amendments and even fresh proposals could be originated in the Assembly; but either tidily drafted bills, or at least a statement of the situation that had arisen, were produced by this Council of five hundred average Athenians, a working committee of the Sovereign People. The establishment of the Council was, in fact, old Solon's chief contribution to the establishment of democracy. For lack of such a working preparatory committee, the Roman Assembly—in theory, under the middle Republic, equally sovereign—was impotent in practice, and the control of current business fell into the hands of a council of ex-magistrates like the Areopagus: the Roman Senate.

The Council in turn had its standing sub-committee, the fifty councillors of each tribe in turn holding this position for a tenth of the year. This period came to be called a Prytany, the councillors of the tribe "in office" being called the Prytaneis, or Presidents. One of them, chosen by lot, took office every evening at sunset, as chairman for twenty-four hours, during which he held the Great Seal of the state, and the keys of the temples in which the archives, gold and silver reserve, and other treasures of the city were kept. This office was never held more than once by the same citizen. The chairman and one-third of the Prytaneis, chosen by him, had to remain during the whole of the twenty-four hours in their official quarters in the Tholos or "Round House," next to the Council Chamber, and it was to them that despatches, official correspondence, ambassadors, or any news of urgent public importance were first brought. It then lay with the Prytaneis to convoke the Council and Assembly, to inform or send for the generals, or to take such other action as might be necessary. The Prytaneis prepared the order-paper (*programma*) for the Council, and the Council for the Assembly. In an emergency this could be very quickly done; a mere statement of the situation that had arisen would be all that was required, followed by the reading of any written message received, or the introduction of the envoys or messengers. After that, the routine question was "who wishes to speak?" and the orators whom Demos was willing to hear, some of them generals or ex-generals, some of them simply popular leaders—"demagogues"—holding no official position, continued the proceedings. The agenda for the regular meetings must often have been quite complicated, often including complete drafts of fairly detailed bills. We have the texts of many such bills, which the Assembly, judging them important, ordered to be engraved on stone for permanent record; they include such diverse items as financial business, treaties, regulation of the affairs of League cities, votes of thanks or honours to individuals or foreign communities, public works, the charter of a colony, or the endowment of a priesthood. Amendments generally begin: "In other respects, as proposed by the Council; but . . ."

Apart from this preparation of business for the Assembly, the Council was charged with a mass of work (steadily increasing as life and finance became more complex), in the supervision of officials and the five-weekly audit of their accounts, in readiness for the Grand Session of the Assembly (once in each Prytany) at which, if all went well, the people formally approved the actions of the Council. At the same session (in later days, and probably in Pericles' time, too) the questions of the food situation and the defence of the country were formally raised, so that the people might periodically review these vital matters without waiting for a crisis to develop. The Council had also to examine the successful candidates for the archonships and other offices now filled by lot, satisfying itself that there was nothing against them, and to require an account of their stewardship from outgoing magistrates and boards, including the Council of the previous year. At the time with which we are now dealing, it could try and punish delinquent magistrates and sundry other offenders against the state, even with death in some cases; this was probably one of the powers transferred from the Areopagus to the Council of Five Hundred by Ephialtes' reform; but within the next twelve years the people, ever jealous of entrusting too great powers to one body, reduced the Council's judicial power to that of committing for trial before an ordinary jury those against whom it was found that there was a *prima facie* case. Altogether, it is not surprising to find that the Council met daily, except on holy days.

The juries, to whom the fall of the Areopagus had brought a great access of importance, were drawn from a panel of several thousand citizens over the age of thirty, attracted (first, it appears, under an Act proposed by Pericles) by a modest payment of two obols (a third of a drachma) per session from the State. Solon, over a hundred years ago, had been the father of these courts, too, when he gave the people the right of requiring an account of their acts from outgoing magistrates. He probably also regularised the right of appeal to the people from a magistrate's judicial sentence. The Sovereign People assembled for judicial purposes was called the Heliaia or Haliaia, an archaic word which in some other states meant the political assembly. As business increased, the Heliaia was divided into juries, empanelled and re-empanelled daily by lot, in order to prevent bribery by ensuring that no citizen could know the composition of the court that was to try his case. Juries consisted of 501 members in most cases, 1,001 or even 1,501 in some big political trials. The jurors were mostly elderly men, for two obols a day (and not every day) made little appeal to the young and vigorous. President of each court was usually an archon; but he was purely a chairman and responsible for preparing the case for trial and keeping reasonable order. There was no advice to the jury on points of law, and the juries, though they were seldom corrupt and, being Greeks, were far from unintelligent, were notoriously apt to be swayed by prejudice, reflecting only too faithfully—as Pericles himself once found—the state of public opinion at the passing hour.

The juries were the Heliaia, and the Heliaia was the Sovereign People. Consequently an appeal lay to a jury in all cases of any importance, and *from* the sentence of a jury, as of the sovereign power, there was no appeal. Only if one could obtain a conviction for perjury—if one could prove, that is, that the Sovereign People had been misinformed—might a case be reopened.

The point of transferring the final verdict on officials from the Council to a jury was simply that the people disliked letting any final decision remain outside its own control and in that of an organised body, even of a year's duration, which might develop a separate *esprit-de-corps*. The juries, re-formed for every case, were open to no such objection.

One exception to the competence of the juries always remained. Charges of wilful murder, poisoning, and arson were always tried before the body of ex-archons, the Areopagus. Conservatism, much tinged with primitive superstition, played a great part in this; the court of the Areopagus was of immemorial antiquity, and said to have been established by the Goddess Athene herself. The feeling that blood-guilt was a pollution always remained strong and the procedure in homicide cases archaic. Also, homicide was never treated at Athens as an offence against the state; it was an offence against the individual, and the prosecutor had to be the next-of-kin, not "any citizen who chose," as in many other cases.

Among executive officers, the Nine Archons had inevitably, since they ceased to be elected, lost much of their prestige. The "Eponymous Archon," or Regent, still gave his name to the year (from midsummer to midsummer) and swore on entering office that all men should hold to the end of his tenure the property they held at its opening, "as in the days of Akastos," the prehistoric king in whose time the Regency was set up; but his chief functions now were to administer legal business concerning property and the family, and to preside, as titular head of the state, at the more modern religious festivals, including the great dramatic festivals of the wine-god. The "King" presided over the more ancient festivals, as he had done since time immemorial, and also over trials involving religious pollution—homicide trials before the Areopagus (formerly the King's privy council) and trials for offences against religion before a jury, as later in the case of Socrates. The "War-Lord" presided over law-suits where either party was a foreigner, and offered the ancient sacrifices to the war-god and to

Artemis of the Wild—the goddess of the wild frontier-country. The six junior archons presided over the remaining jury-courts.

There was also an ever-increasing number of financial, economic, and police officials: port-controllers, market-controllers, inspectors of weights and measures, pay-masters, receivers of taxes, and so on. Among them the board of ten Treasurers of the Goddess ranked high; they were the keepers, jointly with the Council, of the bullion-reserve, and were still chosen from among the richest class of citizens only—both so that they might be less open to temptation, and so that, if any regrettable delinquency occurred, the Treasurers might have some property on which the republic might distrain. But even more important than these, throughout Pericles' career, were the ten Hellenotamiai ("Treasurers of the Greeks"), who received the contributions of the League cities to the treasury at Delos.

Amid the tendency to substitute the drawing of lots for direct election, an exception was always made where expert knowledge was required; notably for some of the chief finance officials and the ten generals; and in a state which was almost continuously at war, the generals, directly elected, often even re-elected, and trusted in so far as Demos, on principle, trusted anyone, rapidly became the leading ministers of the state. Theirs was the office to which not only a Kimon but an Ephialtes inevitably aspired; and no voice was more likely to gain a hearing in the Assembly than theirs, not only on military matters but on high policy generally. But their position differed fundamentally from that of modern cabinet ministers, to whom one instinctively compares them. First, they were not elected on a party "ticket" but individually; and though more radicals might be elected one year and more conservatives another, it remained customary to find men of varying views serving as generals together. This was not felt to matter, since the primary business of generals was not to make policy, but to carry it out. A general might even be ordered to conduct a campaign which he considered unsound; he could express his views in the Assembly, but if the people were bent on a particular conquest, the most that would be likely to happen was that his forces would be increased, or some of his colleagues, if they were more willing, might be entrusted with the mission instead. A general (the second great difference from a modern minister) was not expected to, indeed could hardly, resign rather than carry out a policy of which he disapproved. To do so, or even to show himself unenthusiastic too often, would have been construed as showing cowardice or a lack of loyalty to the people; and with that, unless events later showed him to have been right, a general's public career would be at an end.

Thirdly, the generals had no official duties in connection with the work of the Assembly. Unless the Council or Assembly called upon him for a report or an opinion, each general had exactly the same rights in the Assembly as any other citizen; he had one vote, and the right to speak if the Assembly chose to listen. Naturally the generals could always ask the Council to call the Assembly, and to place on the order-paper business which they wished to raise; but they were not the only leading politicians. In addition to politicians who frequently held office as generals or treasurers, there were other politicians who did not, but were simply leaders or mouthpieces of popular opinion: in the Greek term, demagogues.

Demagogues represented especially the city population of Athens, which not only probably outnumbered the peasant farmers, but could more easily attend the Assembly. Those of whom we know are always drawn from the commercial classes. As such, there was regularly a certain tension between them and the generals, of whom a suprisingly high proportion were members of the old landed families who, like Kimon and Pericles, had accepted the democracy, not unmoved by pride in its military achievements and new imperial power. Demos kept a tight rein on these aristocratic servants of his. Their work—in the next century and perhaps in this—had to be formally "approved" every thirty-six days at the Grand Session of the Assembly, and if it were "disapproved," then the general in question was deposed, and might be put on trial, as happened to Pericles in the last crisis of his life.

The generals, for their part, in addition to much office-work at home, were expected to *lead* their troops in battle. An extraordinarily high proportion of those whose names are known to us were killed in action in fifth-century wars. It was no easy post to be a general at Athens.

Such was the democracy in which Pericles, after the assassination of Ephialtes, played the leading part. He had two separate functions. First, he was one of the most popular speakers in the Assembly—so much so that, with his usual long-headedness, he took to restraining himself from speaking on minor matters, lest people should get tired of him. Unless the matter at issue were one worthy of his personal intervention, he let a friend or supporter express his views. Secondly, he was one of the men frequently elected general; not every year—that would have been no more normal than for a Roman general to be consul every year; though, as there were ten Athenian generals and only two consuls, repeated generalships at Athens were more frequent. Probably Pericles did not even stand for election every year, on the same principle as that of not speaking too often.

When he was general, he threw himself into what others might find the tedious work of an office with the same fiery energy that he had shown on campaigns as a soldier. People said that he was never to be seen in any street of Athens but those which lay between his home and the government offices; that he was never seen at a party in many years, except when his cousin Euryptolemos, the son of Megakles, was married—and even then he only stayed until the first toasts. No doubt there was the usual cheerful exaggeration in such gossip; but no doubt also the social life of his youth had to go by the board. There is no reason to suppose that he missed it. He was thirty-five by now; and in the affairs of the state and the conversation of a group of intimate friends who came to his home, he found life full enough. Among these friends were Damon, the music-master; Sophocles, fast establishing himself as the favourite dramatist of Athens; Anaxagoras, the astronomer and philosopher, and (to the surprise of some Greeks) a sculptor named Pheidias, a humble craftsman who worked with his hands.

By this time, too—probably soon after he was thirty, according to the usual custom—Pericles had married, and had by now two small sons. He named the first Xanthippos, after his father, and the second Paralos, "Coast-dweller," which both suggested interest in the navy (it was the name of one of the two "sacred" galleys of state) and also recalled the name of the constitutional-progressive or "centre" party of the Coast-dwellers, which Pericles' great-grandfather Megakles had led a hundred years ago. Pericles did not bother much about his children, however, leaving them to the women and, as they grew older, to slave attendants or *paidagogoi*—"pedagogues." His ideas on this subject were completely those of his age, which regarded small children as a bore—a troublesome but necessary prelude to the desired possession of grown-up sons. Besides, Pericles was busy. . . .

Neither did his wife play any significant part in the full and absorbing life that he lived among his few men friends and a horde of political and public acquaintances and comrades-in-arms. We do not even know her name. If Plutarch is right in saying that she had already been married to Hipponikos, son of Kallias the Rich, she was probably a near kinswoman of Pericles, and an heiress; for by Athenian law a woman who had no brother had necessarily to marry her nearest male relative—divorcing a previous husband, if any—so that her father's property might descend within his own patrilinear clan. In any case, Pericles' marriage was a loveless business. His wife could be no companion to him; for noble Athenian ladies were little educated and kept in almost Oriental seclusion. Having done his duty by raising a couple of sons, Pericles, by mutual consent, divorced her, so that she could marry or re-marry Hipponikos, to whom she bore another Kallias, rather younger than Pericles' sons. Pericles was to pay dearly for his own or his society's shortcomings in later years.

Nor had Pericles yet a *maîtresse en titre*. Life was too full. The years 460 to 454 were years of astonishing achievement, of victories by land and sea; and as that phrase shows, which Thucydides quotes from a speech of Pericles' old age, the object of his most abiding love was Athens.

Chapter 5

The Years of Conquest

THE FALL of Kimon thus made no immediate difference
to the two leading features of Athenian policy: consolida-
tion of the Delian League, and war with Persia. There
was no clean sweep of Kimon's colleagues; if they were
loyal to the democracy, no one at Athens could have seen
any reason why there should be; and among Pericles' colleagues in the next five years there continued to figure
prominently Myronides and Leokrates, who had been
generals under Aristeides in the Persian War. There was
never any serious attempt to restore the Areopagus, whose
lost powers were too obviously an anachronism when
wielded by an assembly of land-owning mediocrities owing
their position to the luck of the draw; and the veteran
Æschylus, in his last great trilogy, the *Agamemnon* plays,
pleaded for moderation and reconciliation, in his usual
topical allusions. He celebrated, in *The Furies* (which he
must have been composing in 460-459 for performance
in 458), the divine establishment of the Areopagus *as a
court to try homicide,* precisely the function that the
democrats had not taken away; and he also took the
opportunity to introduce some lines in celebration of the
alliance with Argos.

Though he might be approaching seventy, there was
nothing senile about Æschylus. He was as daring and
experimental as ever; indeed, in the same play he made
his chorus of Furies, the demon Avengers of Blood, so
horrible and, so to say, realistic that they caused a panic
in the theatre.

Æschylus' attitude to the politics of 460 was typical
of the landed gentry of his day; even of the old "Marathon fighters" who had followed Aristeides. Aristeides,
and now Pericles, had won them over to democracy—all

but a few. There were secret societies, like that which had compassed the murder of Ephialtes; men prepared, if the chance should offer, even to "sell out" to Sparta; but the majority, like Pericles and the many aristocrats— even clansmen of Kimon—whom we shall find serving with him, had accepted the new order. Pericles' own example must have influenced many. It was to take a decade of disaster, long after Pericles' death, to give oligarchy even a brief and fleeting success in Athens.

With Thasos and the ill-starred attempt to help Sparta "liquidated," the Persian War could now be resumed where the Eurymedon had left it. In 460 or 459, a full League fleet of 200 galleys once more set sail for Cyprus, to root out the Phœnician cities in that mainly Hellenic island.

Then two things happened—both, as it seemed, gifts of the gods to Athens. Megara, hard pressed in war by Corinth, and seeing that Sparta with the Helot war on her hands was in no position to call her allies to order, applied for Athenian protection; and in Egypt a Libyan chief named Inaros raised the Delta country in revolt against Persia. The Athenians with their superb self-confidence, for which no undertaking seemed too ambitious, grasped both opportunities.

Inaros' appeal for help came to the fleet when it had already reached Cyprus. Such a chance seemed too good to miss; and the generals sailed for the Nile with their whole force. Routing a Phœnician squadron in a battle on the Nile, they pushed up the river, joined hands with Inaros, helped him to capture Memphis, the capital (near modern Cairo), and sat down to a long siege of its citadel, the White Castle, while part of the fleet raided Phœnicia, the base of the enemy's naval power.

At home, the Assembly accepted Megara's application, and Athenian troops garrisoned Megara and Pagai, its western port. For the first time Athens controlled a port on the western sea—a source of high hopes for those who already dreamed of making her as powerful in the west of the Greek world as she already was in the east of it. The generals' chief anxiety was lest Megara, which was a good mile from the sea, might be cut off by enemy land forces. The solution adopted was to build a pair of parallel walls from Megara to the harbour of Nisaia, opposite Salamis, and to garrison them—with Athenians. The idea, once projected, was obviously a good one, for Greek armies, especially Spartans, were absolutely impotent against stone walls. Not long afterwards the Athenians started the far greater enterprise of building their own "long walls" from the city down to Piræus and Phaleron, distances of five and three miles respectively, to secure for the city something like the advantages of an island position.

The alliance with Megara meant war with Corinth— once friendly to Athens as a counterpoise to Aigina, but henceforth a bitter and dogged enemy. While Sparta's hands were full, it seemed to Athens also a good opportunity to try to control the Argolic peninsula, which would give short and secure communication with friendly Argos itself. Troizen, on the tip of the peninsula, connected with Athens by old ties of friendship, came into her alliance during these years if not before; and in 459 an Athenian squadron rounded Cape Skyllaion and attacked Halieis, "the Fishermen," a little town on the south coast with a fine harbour. The operation miscarried, however; the enemy had evidently got wind of the expedition, and the landing-party was driven off by troops from Epidauros and Corinth.

This move brought Epidauros into the war. This important secondary state clung firmly to her alliance with Sparta and Corinth out of fear of her neighbour, Argos. Lying as it did on the shortest route between Argos and Athens, the town became the objective of repeated Athenian and Argive attacks, but held out stubbornly against them.

The next episode was a naval engagement in the Saronic Gulf between the Corinthians and the Athenian home fleet; an Athenian victory, in spite of the absence of probably a good hundred Athenian first-line ships with the League fleet in Egypt; and at this, Aigina, her government evidently realising that her opportunity to break Athens' grip on the gulf was now or never, joined Corinth and Epidauros. Athens in turn called in contingents from her allies; it is significant that she could still rely on their loyalty, under the democratic governments which she fostered, for a war against Greeks. It was a struggle of united Ionian versus Dorian sea-power; and in a pitched battle off Aigina the Athenians won a sweeping victory, capturing seventy ships, and following up their success by landing troops on Aigina to blockade the town. Corinth and Epidauros tried to reinforce Aigina, but the Athenians, led by Leokrates, moved so fast that only three hundred managed to slip across before the blockade was complete. The time to deal with Pericles' "eyesore of Piræus" had come at last.

Crippled at sea, the Corinthians struck back on land, at the only point possible—at Megara; hoping that, with the great armament still away in Egypt, the Athenians would at least have to withdraw Leokrates' army from Aigina to save their ally. But the Athenians did nothing of the kind. Their last reserves—boys of eighteen and nineteen, veterans between fifty and sixty, men hitherto left at home as unfit or on civil duties, everyone who could carry a shield in battle—marched to Megara under Athens' other great veteran general, Myronides. Joining these to the troops of Megara, Myronides beat off the Corinthian attack; and the Corinthians, foiled in their desire to besiege Megara or devastate its olive-groves, picked up their dead and retired home. When they had gone, the Athenians, left in possession of the field, and considering rightly that they had won a strategic victory, set up a trophy, according to Greek custom; but this was not the end of the matter. The Corinthians on their return found themselves the victims of such barbed taunts from their old fathers and uncles, as having been repulsed by an army of dotards and babies, that after about twelve days they decided that they had not been defeated, and would go back and set up a trophy to prove it. The result was disastrous; for the Athenians burst out from Megara against them, cut down the men who were in the act of erecting the trophy, assailed the rest, who had not been expecting a battle, and drove them away in rout on the road to Corinth. Nor was this the worst; for a large party of them took a wrong turning and found themselves in a cul-de-sac: a piece of private ground surrounded by a ditch and having no other exit. Myronides promptly blocked the entrance with his spearmen and surrounded the place with his light-armed troops, who shot down the whole force with slingstones and arrows; a serious blow to Corinth's limited manpower.

After this, the Athenians garrisoned the passes of Geraneia against any future threat from the Peloponnese.

It had been a wonderful year, but the casualties, in the aggregate, were fairly serious. At the end of the campaigning season the tribe Erechtheïs set up, in proud sorrow, its own separate war-memorial (an unusual proceeding). The stone reads: "Of Erechtheïs these died in war, in Cyprus, in Egypt, in Phœnicia, at Halieis, at Aigina, and at Megara, i n t h e s a m e y e a r." The last words are spaced out for emphasis. There follows a list of 177 names, including two generals, a formidable total for one tribal regiment in a year with no serious reverse.

The following year saw far more serious fighting; for Sparta herself was now ready to take a hand. The Helot revolt was still dragging on, but the rebels had been driven back into their fastness in the great mountain amphitheatre of Ithome, and she could spare troops for a campaign abroad. She was not yet formally at war with Athens, however, and her generals were far too good soldiers to run their heads against a stone wall in the passes of Geraneia. If Athens chose to support Argos in threatening Sparta's primacy in the Peloponnese, Sparta could give Athens something to think about elsewhere.

A pretext was given by an invasion of the little state of Doris, west of Thermopylæ—traditionally the mother-country of the Spartans themselves—by its more powerful neighbours the Phokians. One of their three chief villages had already fallen when the Dorians sent a piteous appeal to their powerful "colonists." Sparta assembled a force far larger than was necessary—10,000 allies, with 1,500 Spartiates and Lakonians—and sent it over by sea under Nikomedes, son of Kleombrotos, uncle and guardian of the young king Pleistoanax.

That this meant trouble was not lost on the Athenians. They sent fifty galleys to the Corinthian Gulf—enough to sink any fleet that Sparta's allies could still raise, and the first Athenian warships to be seen on the west coast of Greece; and they blocked the mountain passes on the Spartans' way home by Plataia and Megara. The scope of operations was widening.

Phokis sued for peace, and Nikomedes showed some more of his hand. He marched through Phokis into Boiotia and proceeded to restore Thebes—in disgrace since her support of the Persians twenty years before—to her old position as president of the Boiotian League. Thebes, her aristocracy compromised by the discredited pro-Persian policy, seems to have been democratic at this time, though no doubt in a more "agrarian" and less thoroughgoing manner than Athens; but the Spartans could not help that. Reasons of state demanded a strong Boiotia, and if (now as in the following century) the centralising parties in Boiotia were democratic, so it must be. If Athens could find allies in pro-Persian Thessaly and Argos, then Sparta could do the same by Thebes. Moreover, there were men in Athens, of the extreme reactionary party, who were ready to open the gates to a Spartan army some dark night, if only they might thus get the government put back into their own hands and stop the building of the Long Walls, which meant to them the confirmation for ever of the supremacy of the sailors and traders over the landed interest. Sheering off from an attack on the Athenians in the mountain passes, Nikomedes marched into south-eastern Boiotia, whence the way into Attica was easier and whence he threatened Euboia.

But the Athenians, as in the days of Marathon, had determined not to stand passive and perhaps be betrayed, but themselves to take the offensive. To some sanguine spirits, indeed, it seemed that this enemy force, cut off from home, was lingering merely out of doubt what to do next, and that a bold attack might destroy it. They had still troops away in Egypt and at Aigina; but on Aigina island the besieging army must by now have been "dug in" in fortified blockading lines, which could be more lightly held. Calling in allies from all sides—1,000 Argives with some men of their allied state, Kleonai, a force of the fine cavalry of Thessaly, islanders and Ionians of the League—Pericles and his colleagues raised an army 14,000 strong (counting, as was usual, armoured men only) and marched via Dekeleia to seek out the enemy.

As they camped in the territory of Tanagra, the nearest Boiotian city, a man came to the Athenian outposts asking for speech with the generals. It was the exiled Kimon, asking to be allowed to fight as an ordinary citizen soldier in the ranks of his tribe. He must have been living as near as was permitted, probably in Euboia, and he had already sent in his offer to the Council at Athens. It was the offer of an honest patriot; but to the democrats it was embarrassing. How did Kimon and his friends stand with regard to the suspected reactionary conspiracy? As there was presumably no time to lay the matter before the Assembly, the Council instructed the generals to refuse the offer. Not without embarrassment in their turn, Pericles and his colleagues ordered Kimon out of the lines. Kimon left, with the parting message to his friends and supporters, to play the man for Athens.

Near Tanagra the armies met, and there was prolonged, savage, and bloody fighting. Pericles, who had already a reputation for gallantry, surpassed himself this day in reckless self-exposure. He at least had a bad conscience about the rebuff to Kimon. Kimon's supporters, too, fought with furious courage, mindful of their leader's message, and eager to wipe away the suspicion of disloyalty. Yet in spite of all, Nikomedes' smaller but more homogeneous army, probably reinforced by Boiotians, on the whole held its own. Towards evening the combatants seem to have separated; and then something happened which turned the scale. The Thessalians, feudal cavalry as they were, led by aristocrats sympathetic to Sparta, went over to the enemy, and made a sudden and treacherous attack on the great mule train that carried the

Athenian army's supplies. There was panic and massacre in the gathering dusk; then the Athenians came to the rescue; and then the Poloponnesians, who had presumably concerted this move with the Thessalian chieftains, came up to intervene.

By daylight, things were still undecided, and the grim hammer-and-tongs battle was resumed; but the Athenians and their allies must have been drawn by the attack on the convoy on to ground of their antagonists' choice. Fighting bravely and not in rout, but with heavy losses, they were driven from the field.

Over a hundred of the friends of Kimon had died for Athens and for their leader's good name. The Argive and Kleonaian contingents had been terribly cut up: their casualty-list, fragments of which have been found inscribed on stone among the war-memorials of Athens, seems to have room for something like 400 names. There is no record of the total casualties. But the Peloponnesians had paid heavily too. Nikomedes did not attempt an invasion of Attica. He marched back to the western passes, unguarded now, passed through the Megarid, where his men relieved their feelings by some destruction of the vines and olive trees of the hapless Megarians, and dismissed his contingents to their homes.

The Athenians, indomitable as ever, were already planning the next move.

The friends of Kimon had rehabilitated themselves with their blood and Pericles himself now proposed a decree, by which, as in the days of Xerxes' invasion, the "ostracised" leader was recalled from exile. By Kimon's influence with Sparta, it might be possible to put an end to hostilities; and a truce of four months was arranged, during which Kimon probably hoped to reach a lasting agreement. But the armistice said nothing about Boiotia; and just sixty-two days after the defeat at Tanagra, Myronides with the whole available land army marched again by the same road as before. At the village of Oinophyta ("the Vineyards") he met and overthrew the Boiotians in one of the most decisive victories of Athenian arms. Tanagra fell, and had her fortifications razed, that she might no longer be a stronghold in Boiotia's eastern gate; and then Myronides marched through the country, where city after city surrendered, becoming an ally of Athens and abjuring the newly restored hegemony of Thebes. This, it appears—though one must add that the evidence either way is extremely sketchy—involved relying on the local separatist parties, which were also conservative parties, led by the squires; strange allies for democratic Athens; but for Athens, as lately for Sparta, imperial policy seems to have made strange bedfellows. Thebes alone, still under her "peasant party" democracy, may have stood out of the Athenian alliance; Athenians may have hoped that the fear of Thebes would keep the lesser cities loyal, just as the fear of Argos had long kept Corinth and Epidauros staunch allies of Sparta.

Beyond Boiotia the mountaineers of Phokis, smarting under their coercion by Sparta, joined the Athenian alliance, and the eastern Lokrians on the coast, whose territory stretched up to Thermopylæ, were forced to do likewise, a hundred of their leading men being taken as hostages. In one campaign Athens had brought into her orbit the whole of central Greece.

The winter's armistice with Sparta petered out without leading to a peace or even being renewed. The Athenians, flushed with victory, were no doubt, as in many negotiations, indisposed to make any concessions. They finished the Long Walls in the same winter (457-456?) and Athens was thus invulnerable to anything that Sparta could do so long as Athens ruled the sea. The siege of Aigina was also drawing to a close. Starved out, the islanders surrendered, agreeing to the breaching of their walls and the confiscation of their fleet, and to joining the League with the heavy tribute of thirty talents a year. Athens also strengthened her hold on the Corinthian Gulf by the capture (just when is uncertain) of the Lokrian port of Naupaktos, near the gulf's western "narrows," and when the Messenian insurgents on Mount Ithome at last came to terms with Sparta on condition that they should be allowed to depart from the Peloponnese, the Athenians settled them here, where they proved staunch, vigorous, and extremely useful allies.

Sparta, relieved of this thorn in her flesh, might have been expected to resume the offensive; especially as a Persian agent, one Megabazos, well supplied with gold, had managed to slip across the Ægean, with instructions to spare no expense in stirring up the Peloponnesians to invade Attica. He was now at Sparta, where his "bakshish" found ready acceptance; but no invasion resulted. Spartan manpower was still weak after the earthquake; and in 455 the Athenians gave her other things to think about. The rising Athenian general Tolmides sailed right round the Peloponnese, harrying the coast of Lakonia, and even captured and burned the Spartan naval port of Gythion, slipping away before the enemy could concentrate against him. Then, passing up the west coast, he enrolled the islanders of Zakynthos as allies, captured the Corinthian colony of Chalkis, west of Naupaktos, made alliance with, or at least an impression on, the Akarnanians north-west of the gulf and the Achaians south of it, and ended by landing his troops and defeating the men of Sikyon, Corinth's western neighbour, hitherto out of reach of Athens' long arm. He then probably laid up his ships at Pagai (where Athens certainly had a powerful squadron a little later), and marched his crews home by land.

Athens was in a fair way to encircle Sparta and bottle her up in the southern Peloponnese. With Troizen, Argos, Zakynthos, Achaia, and Megara as allies, the next task was to overwhelm the isthmus states around Corinth, Sparta's one remaining "window" to the north; hence the Athenian attacks on Sikyon and Epidauros, aiming at weakening Corinth by "knocking away the props"; while Sparta, baffled and discredited, could be kept in check, it seemed, by Argos alone.

Meanwhile the home politics of Athens had not stood still. Pericles, who, after his early soldiering was now becoming increasingly interested in home affairs, took a leading part in a series of measures which carried on and completed the development of the democracy. In the year after Oinophyta the chief archonships, hitherto still confined to "knights," were thrown open by law to the next taxation class, the "small-holders" (Zeugitai, or "Owners of a yoke of oxen"); and in practice, before many years had passed, even the poorest, officially classified as Labourers (Thetes), were accepted as candidates if they wished to stand, merely being put down officially as "Small-holders." But of greater real importance was the development, always associated with Pericles' name, of the principle of payment to citizens for doing the work of the state.

When this was introduced is uncertain. Councillors, who gave up the best of their time for a whole year, may well have been paid even earlier. Archons, if poor men were to hold these positions, also clearly had to be paid. But what was revolutionary in Pericles' reform was, in particular, the new payment for service on juries (see above, p. 65).

None of Pericles' measures gets a worse "Press" from the later Greek philosophical and literary tradition. By it, we are told, Pericles began the transformation of the virile "men of Marathon" into dole-fed idlers, only interested in gossip and the latest news, hangers around the market-place and law courts, listening greedily to demagogues—instead, one seems to read between the lines, of leaving public affairs to their betters, for whom such occupations were, of course, appropriate, since their work was done for them by their farm-labourers and slaves. Gossip said that the idea originally came to Pericles from Damon, and that the measure was a party move; "bribing the people with the public funds" in Damon's reputed phrase, and thereby outbidding the lavish generosity of Kimon; and there may have been an element of truth in this, for with Kimon at home again, arguing for peace with Sparta and regaining popularity by his personality, his use of his "princely" wealth, and the memory of his friends' loyal sacrifice at Tanagra, there was need for a radical leader not to stand still. But in fact Pericles had better reasons than these for pressing on with such a policy.

The importance of the step lay in the fact that the great

juries of hundreds of citizens—*ad hoc* committees of the sovereign people, as we have called them—now not only dealt with Athenian litigation and scrutinised the accounts of officials if these were queried; they also handled an increasing amount of business from the League. As a matter of administration, an increasing number of jury-man-days was wanted; it was necessary ultimately to re-cruit as many as 6,000 jurors. As a matter of party politics, if the government of the people was really to be carried on by the people and for the people, it was es-sential that the mass of the people, the poor as well as the leisured minority, should be able to take their turn in supervising what was done.

In some other Greek constitutions, which were reck-oned democratic, but less radical and more respectable in later philosophers' eyes than Athens, they followed a different and, to the minds of these philosophers, a more excellent way. No one was paid for doing adminstrative or judicial work; those who did not do it when the duty came their way were fined; but the fines were graded ac-cording to property, or the poor were excused altogether. Those on whom the lot fell to serve as judges or council-lors were allowed to swear an oath that private affairs did not admit of their serving—but not if they belonged to one of the higher-income groups; or the comfortably-off were compelled on pain of a fine to serve on juries, while the poor were not; or in some states, any citizen could register for attendance in the Assembly and on juries, but having registered, if he failed to attend he was fined. This naturally acted as a deterrent to poor men. Similarly, legislation sometimes compelled the well-to-do, but not the poor, to provide themselves with armour and weap-ons, and to keep themselves physically fit by regular exer-cises. What could be more humane? . . . But Aristotle—the real Aristotle of the *Politics,* to whom we owe these details—at once clearer-sighted and more candid than the author of the *Athenian Constitution,* summarises all these practices as "the devices by which oligarchies deceive the people."

Payment of jurymen, councillors, and archons was, in

fact, as necessary to the working of city-state democracy as the payment of members of parliament to a parliamentary democracy; while in its social bearing it has been compared to an old-age pension.

One step, known to later Athenian democracy, Periclean Athens did not take: that of payment for attendance at meetings of the Assembly. The result was that for routine meetings, if business was not going to be exciting, the attendance was often very thin indeed. Six thousand —at a time when Athens had quite sixty thousand adult male citizens—was, in fact, a good attendance. To collect a reasonable sample of the sovereign people on a dull day, Athens consequently had recourse to one of those humorous dodges dear to Greek legislation. The Scythian slave police were sent out to "sweep" the streets near Parliament Hill, carrying ropes, red and dripping with wet vermilion dye. The tradesman in his little shop was not molested, but anyone out in the streets was thus physically urged to do his duty by turning up for parliament; and anyone who while trying to escape the cordon got a touch of the wet paint on his clothes, became not only a source of public merriment but liable to a fine.

Apart from the war, other foreign affairs were constantly preoccupying the Assembly at this time; both those of the League, which was coming to look more and more like an Athenian empire, and those of the ever-widening circle of independent states that sought Athens' support in troubles with their neighbours. It was in the year of Oinophyta, according to the recent conclusions of American epigraphists, that the Assembly gave a sympathetic hearing to an embassy from so far off as western Sicily, where the non-Greek city of Egesta was being threatened by the Dorian Greek colonists of Selinous—natural allies of Athens' enemies in the Peloponnese. A treaty of alliance, couched in general terms, was concluded, part of whose text survives. Themistocles in his time had had his western dreams, and this was a natural result of Athens' new interests in the Corinthian Gulf; but it was also a pointer towards what Athens a generation later was to find very perilous seas.

Far away in Persia King Artaxerxes, finding no satisfaction in the reports of what Megabazos was doing with his money, recalled the ambassador with his depleted money-bags. In 455 he was reported building up an army in Syria under one of his best generals, Megabyxos; but it was so long since Persian arms had effected anything against Greeks that no one at Athens can have felt any qualms when, in 454, a League squadron of fifty galleys sailed for the Nile to relieve part of the force which was still supporting the Egyptians' extremely desultory blockade of the White Castle. Even when the ships due home were long delayed, there was probably little anxiety. And then, late in the year, came the terrible news that Megabyxos had succeeded in his invasion of Egypt, with the help of a Phœnician fleet which had penetrated the Delta. He had relieved the White Castle; he had besieged the late besiegers on an island at the head of the Delta; and at last by a fine feat of engineering had diverted the water from the channel in front of that island, and taken it by storm. The general, Charitimides, had fallen with many of his men; and it was only a remnant which, after a desperate resistance, retired from Egypt under a convention and, after a grim desert march, reached Cyrene. Inaros, the insurgent chief, was captured soon afterwards, and it was only in parts of the Delta—much of it then trackless fen—that some of the warlike marsh-men kept up the fight.

To complete the disaster, the relieving squadron sailed unsuspecting up the eastern branch of the Nile and was surprised, apparently at a camp on shore, by the Persians from the land side and their Phœnician allies on the river; and of this force also only a fraction fought its way out of the trap.

The great epoch of Athenian conquests had come to an end.

Chapter 6

The Years of Crisis (1)

THE EGYPTIAN DISASTER almost coincided in time with
the return of an expedition under Myronides from Thessaly—the farthest northward fling of an Athenian land
army. Myronides had been directed to restore to his
native Pharsalos an exiled prince, Orestes; a blow at the
aristocrats who had played Athens false at Tanagra. He
had a large army, including thousands of Boiotian and
Phokian allies. But he was baffled on the plains of Thessaly by the mounted noblemen and their retainers, who
swarmed round his outposts and, as Thucydides says,
confined his occupation of territory to the ground his
armoured infantry stood on. Unable to maintain his army
while besieging Pharsalos, Myronides retired, and Thessaly, for some years, had to be "written off" as an ally.

This rebuff, however, involved no such disastrous losses
as the debacle in Egypt. About 200 out of 250 ships had
been lost; [1] their complements totalled anything up to
8,000 soldiers and 32,000 sailors, of whom the great majority perished. Most of these, no doubt, would be allies.
To get the Athenian losses, we must deduct the crews of
allied ships, still numerous (say, 40 per cent) and of
allied sailors (but not soldiers) in Athenian ships; say a
third of their crews. Still, out of some 30,000 lost, at
least 12,000 must have been Athenians. Losses of not
much under 4,000 soldiers ("small-holders") and 10,000
sailors (mostly "labourers") fell upon a population
which, even if larger now than in 431, when we have
figures for armoured men, can hardly have exceeded

[1] Many scholars doubt this, on the grounds that the population of
Athens could not have stood such losses. But this is certainly the
account suggested in Thucydides' introduction, and believed by
Isokrates in the next century.

70,000 men of military age; some good authorities would put it much lower.

Athens was never again to take the offensive simultaneously against Persia and the Peloponnese. As Pericles once said in a funeral oration for a later campaign, "with these young men the spring is gone out of the year."

But Athens was never so indomitable as in defeat. In case of a Phœnician raid on the Ægean, the League treasury was moved from Delos to Athens; a momentous step in the evolution from League to Empire. Athenian officers abroad watched keenly for any signs of disaffection. There was trouble at Miletos, where the oligarchs massacred the democratic leaders and seceded; but by 450 Athens had brought the city to heel again. Meanwhile, in 453, embarking 1,000 armoured troops on the ships at Pagai, Pericles himself set sail to demonstrate Athenian power down the Corinthian Gulf.

Pericles began operations as Tolmides had ended, by descending upon Sikyon, where he routed the home levies at the brook Nemea, and chased them within their walls. He had hoped even to capture the city; but if he was in touch with democrats within, they failed to move, and Peloponnesian troops were marching to the rescue. Pericles set up a trophy for his victory and re-embarked his force in good time. The fleet sailed on, picking up allied troops from the little cities of Achaia, and crossing the Gulf joined Athens' other allies of Akarnania—enemies of Corinth, which had planted colonies on their coast—in an attack on the dissident Akarnanian city of Oiniadai, among the mud-flats of the Acheloos. Oiniadai, a hard place to get at among its water-channels, also held out, and Pericles returned home; whether to Pagai, or whether he now brought most of the western fleet back into the Ægean, does not appear. He had effected nothing, but it had been a successful demonstration, and Pericles' reputation was enhanced by his careful generalship, which had avoided even the smallest regrettable incident throughout the campaign.

Pericles, it is clear, had been deeply affected by the inroads on Athenian manpower, especially the farmer and

middle-class heavy-infantry manpower, made by the war-
fare of the past ten years; Egypt, Tanagra, Leagros' disaster in Thrace, 177 killed from one tribe in a year with no
serious reverse. It was remarked how careful he, once so
reckless of his own life, now was of the lives of his men.
"Depend upon it," he would say, "so far as depends on
me, you are all immortal!" Like Montgomery, he never
engaged in battle without having done all he possibly
could to make victory certain. He never suffered a serious
defeat.

Another source of his popularity was his respect for
his citizen soldiers. "Remember, Pericles," he used to say
to himself; "you are commanding free men, Greeks,
Athenians!" And he applied all his parliamentarian's arts
of leadership to the tricky business—as some generals
found it—of discipline in a democratic army.

The war with the Peloponnesian League dragged on,
without striking incident, now that Athens as well as
Sparta was above all things anxious to avoid losses. The
chief scene of operations in three otherwise blank years
may well have been Argolis, where Argos with Athenian
aid, at some unknown date, beat off a Spartan invasion
on the field of Oinoe. Both sides were war-weary; and at
last, in 451, Sparta concluded a thirty years' peace with
Argos and, through Kimon, a five years' truce with
Athens. Failure to agree on anything more permanent was
no doubt due to Spartan unwillingness formally to acknowledge Athens' new imperial position.

Athens, meanwhile, was consolidating her League into
an Empire. Perhaps as early as 453 she inaugurated a
new system of *clêrûchies* (colonies whose members remained Athenian citizens) at strategic points, when Tolmides led 500 colonists to the important, central, and
once recalcitrant island of Naxos. In the next few years
250 went to Andros, on the route to the Dardanelles; an
unknown number under Tolmides to southern Euboia, on
the other side of the Andros channel; 1,000, under a
treaty with the Thracian tribe of the Bisaltai, to help
secure the northern marches of the peninsula of Chalki-
diké, and another 1,000, conducted by Pericles himself,

to the Gallipoli Peninsula, where they resumed the work done by Kimon's ancestors, repairing the old wall across the Isthmus of Bulair for defence against the warlike tribes outside. The passage of the Dardanelles was now a vital Athenian interest; for the teeming city population was dependent, now that Egypt could no longer be counted on, on corn from the Greek ports and corn-growing Scythian tribes in the black earth belt of the Ukraine.

When Athens took land from Greeks for her colonists, she seems to have paid for it by reducing the local communities' contributions to the League. Andros' tribute was reduced from twelve talents to six in 450–449 B.C.; that of Karystos in southern Euboia from 7½ to five at the same time; Naxos, a much larger island than Andros, is paying only 6⅔ when we first have figures for it in 448; and the Gallipoli cities were still more drastically scaled down after 447. Nevertheless, the islanders resented the *clêrûchies* bitterly. What they wanted was not Athens' idea of justice, but to be left to themselves.

But Athens was no longer attending to what her "allies" might say. The periodical League conferences had lapsed —at latest, when the Treasury was transferred to Athens. The modern theory that that transference itself was proposed by a powerful ally (Samos) is baseless—it rests on a dubious story of a proposal, which was not accepted, over twenty years earlier.

Also, whatever Athens may have been doing in Boiotia, she was showing herself not indifferent to the forms of government of her "allies" in the Ægean. Not everywhere, but certainly in several cities, she intervened to impose her own form of democracy—especially on the coast of Asia Minor, where the danger of a Persian comeback was still a reality. The affair at Miletos had shown what might happen if control was left to unreliable elements; and so, in the civil year 450–449, the Assembly regulated Miletos' constitution according to Athenian ideas. There was similar intervention at an unknown date at the inland Ionian city of Kolophon, and also, now or even earlier, at Erythrai, for which we have enough of the Athenian decree on the subject (though the preamble and date have perished) to give a vivid glimpse of the Athenian Empire at work.

The chief points are:

(1) Religion: Erythrai is required to send offerings to the great quadriennial Athenian state festival. (Nothing could more explicitly emphasise the city's subject status.)

(2) Constitution: Erythrai is provided with a Council closely modelled on that of Athens, though proportionately smaller. (Evidently the Athenians felt that this institution was essential, to prevent oligarchic elements from getting the management of the democracy into their hands.) Councillors are to take an oath of loyalty to the People of Athens and of her Allies, as well as of Erythrai. It also appears from this oath that in certain legal cases (notably those concerning the banishment of political suspects) reference has to be made to the Athenian courts. It transpires also that Erythrai is under Athenian military occupation, and is being visited by an Athenian mission of Inspectors (*episkopoi*—later the Christian word "bishop").

(3) Law: Persons banished from Erythrai for murder will be banished from the whole empire.

The following is a translation. (Words in square brackets are not in the Greek.)

"The Erythraians shall bring all the [usual] sacred victims to the Great Panathenaia, to a value of not less than three minæ [300 drachmas]. The Directors of the Sacrifice shall distribute the meat thereof to those Erythraians who are present, at the rate of one drachma a head. If the sacred victims are brought, but are not of the value of three minæ according to these directions, the Directors of the Sacrifice shall buy victims and charge the cost to the people of Erythrai; and the meat shall be given to whosoever wishes to take it.

"There shall be at Erythrai a Council of a hundred and twenty, chosen by lot; those on whom the lot falls shall undergo scrutiny before the [outgoing] Council of the Erythraians. No man under thirty years of age shall serve; and any candidate found to be disqualified shall be liable to prosecution. No one shall serve twice within four years. On the present occasion the lots shall be supervised and the Council installed by the [Athenian] Inspectors and Garrison Commander, and in future by the [outgoing] Council and the Garrison Commander. Every prospective Councillor, before taking up his duties, shall swear by Zeus and Apollo and Demeter, invoking destruction upon himself and his children if he be false to his oath. Councillors shall administer their business according to the existing laws; for any breach, they shall be liable to a fine up to 1,000 drachmas, and they shall deposit [as surety?] with the People of Erythrai a sum not less.

"The Councillor's oath shall be as follows:

"I will perform my duties as Councillor to the best of my ability, and faithfully to the People of Erythrai and of Athens and of the Allies. I will not revolt from the People of Athens and of the Allies of Athens, nor will permit another so to do. I will not desert [to the Persians], nor will I permit another so to do. I will not receive [into the city] any of those who are in exile among the Persians without the permission of the Athenians and of the People [of Erythrai], nor will I exile any person now dwelling here, except by decision of the Athenians and of the People [of Erythrai].

"If an Erythraian murder an Erythraian, he shall be put to death if the Court so order; and if he be sentenced to banishment, he shall be banished from the whole territory of the Allies of Athens, and his goods shall be forfeit to the People of Erythrai.

"If any person be convicted of conspiracy to betray to the [late] tyrants the City of Erythrai, he shall be outlawed, himself and his children, unless his children furnish proof of their loyalty and demonstrate it to the People of Erythrai and of Athens. [If they do so] and deposit all the property of the condemned, his children shall receive back half thereof, and half shall be confiscated.

"Likewise if anyone be convicted of treason against the People of Athens or [of conspiracy to betray] the garrison at Erythrai . . ."

The rest of the text is fragmentary and indecipherable, except for scattered phrases, including a mention of archers; these may be, as at Athens, Athenian military police.

About the same time the Assembly decreed the extension of Athenian weights, measures, and coinage to the whole Empire and the suppression of local currencies (with certain exceptions, notably the gold pieces of Kyzikos on the Sea of Marmara; Athens herself did not coin gold). It was an extremely sensible economic measure; earlier there had been, for example, not only four independent cities but three independent currencies in the island of Keos alone, with an area much less than that of the county of Rutland; but nothing was more likely to offend local pride and patriotism, even though many of the old currencies had disappeared since the Persian occupation.

Pericles, democrat and even liberal though he was (indeed, the first liberal in history; [2] therein lies his originality), had not the slightest doubt of the propriety of these proceedings. It was so clear to him that Athens led the world in all the arts of civilisation, that Athens, in his own words, was an education to Greece—that he never doubted but that it was Athens' duty to lead politically, too. Most of the inhabitants of "the cities" (as speakers in the Assembly usually called the Empire) still followed Athens willingly, it is clear; Athens, the deliverer both from the Great King of Persia without and from the little tyrants and domestic oligarchies within. If a little coercion was temporarily necessary to break down parochial prejudices in favour of local money, or to see that reactionary elements did not gain political power, then coercion must be applied, until all men, or enough, should see reason. The *clêrûchies* of these years are said to have been his idea, or that of his mentor Damonides. Apart from their strategic importance, they were part of his

[2] A liberal is a person who understands that liberty includes not only his own liberty to do what he likes, but other people's liberty to do what he does not like. Cf. Pericles' remarks in the Funeral Oration, p. 187.

social policy, a measure to plant out any poor Athenian who was able and willing, on a farm of his own.

Whether he was in favour of planting *clêrûchies* in the limited space of the islands, where they produced the maximum of friction for the minimum of land taken, is another matter. Those colonies, we are told—if only by late and bad sources—were Tolmides' work; and Tolmides, the son of Tolmaios (both names mean "the Daring"), was a man who always seems to have striven to live up to his name. He is said to have been "anxious to emulate the fame of Pericles"; and he was the natural leader of those impatient of Pericles' new quadragenarian caution. Pericles had the greater reputation at present, but his position was not unassailable. No man's was, in face of that turbulent Assembly; so he was not only serving Athens but making an adroit move in the parliamentary struggle for popularity, when he, so to speak, outbid Tolmides with a larger *clêrûchy* in the Chersonese, in a place where there was need for it and where there was more room.

But in the year of the truce with Sparta, Pericles was faced with a far graver decision. In spite of the losses in war—which only fell on young men—Athens and Piræus were still crowded; moreover, we must suppose that immigrants still flowed into the capital from the Empire; poor men, mostly, "to seek their fortune," attracted by the easy naturalisation which had been Athens' policy since Kleisthenes. But since Pericles' own institution of payment for civil administration, especially for service on juries, citizenship had been a source, not only of pride and a modest share of power, but of direct financial advantage. There were other benefits, too; for example, if you became an Athenian, and then were killed in Athens' wars, the state would look after your wife and children. In the circumstances, those who had the citizenship already looked with jealous eyes upon immigrants; and a strong movement grew up for restriction of the franchise. The Athenian people had, in fact, become—even the poorest of them—a privileged minority in the Empire.

The antithesis of Empire and democracy has never been more brutally and clearly posed.

There was much that was plausible and even true to be said for restriction. It was argued on the most obvious grounds that there were too many people in the city, in spite of the thousands carried off by *clêrûchies* or war casualties; and on a more refined level it *could* be argued that the whole ancient character of Athens was in danger of being altered by the flood of immigrants. The United States have been faced by the same problem on a vaster scale within this generation.

It was a serious matter to reverse the policy of Kleisthenes. Athens' march towards the leadership of Greece had depended hitherto, not only upon the brilliance of her civilisation and of her generals but, very largely, upon the sheer size of the population that could suffer such casualties year after year and still man 200 ships at a time. Also, it must surely have been clear even before the event, to a man of Pericles' intellect, that the closing of the franchise would strike a serious if not mortal blow at the goodwill still felt towards Athens by the masses in the Empire. But if so, it was also clear to him that this was a reform—if one can use the term of such a piece of arrant reaction—on which Athens was bent; on which the poor citizens, the delighted supporters of Pericles' radical measures, felt at one with, and even more strongly than, the conservatives who looked to Kimon. If Pericles did not propose it, someones else would.

Old Kimon (he was nearing sixty by now) was, in fact, showing signs of "coming back" as a serious political rival. The fact that he, as the man whom Sparta trusted, had had to be employed to make an end of a war that was leading nowhere, had done more for his prestige than anything else since Tanagra. Also, a little paradoxically, the policy of a renewed attack on Persia, which Kimon was eager to lead, was not unpopular. The Levant offered prospects of spoil and easier victories, quite unlike those of a war against the stubborn Peloponnesians; and at Athens (it became painfully clear when peace was restored) war, financed out of Delian League contributions, had become an industry; one might almost say a vested interest.

Meanwhile it was unfortunate for Pericles that in Tolmides a distinguished younger general, with ideas of political leadership, was also coming forward. It would not do to lose the leadership of the Assembly on an important issue just now.

Whatever his private views Pericles, like the Alkmeonid that he was, made his decision. He made a political bargain with Kimon. The initials steps were taken, it is said, once more through Elpinike, whose husband Kallias was a leading politician. Pericles would support Kimon's proposal for a new Levant campaign, and in return Kimon would leave home affairs to Pericles. Pericles then himself proposed to the Council and Assembly the restriction of Athenian citizenship to persons of citizen parentage on both sides. With an absolute minimum of trouble the law was carried. It was a fateful turning-point in Athenian history; one wonders whether Pericles ever regretted it.

In the spring of 450, for the last time, Kimon led a Delian League fleet of 200 ships into the Levant. The first objective was Cyprus. Kimon landed his troops, enlisted the Greek cities as allies, and settled down to besiege the Phœnician stronghold of Kition, the Biblical Kittim. He detached sixty ships once more to support the insurgents in Egypt, where a prince called Amyrtaios was still holding out in the fens; and there seems to have been fighting in Cilicia against Persian land forces too. We know all too little about these major operations; but it is clear that, in spite of some tactical successes, the campaign was a failure. Kition held out with all the stubbornness of Phœnician and Jewish sieges. Food ran short; Kimon himself fell sick; his fellow-general Anaxikrates was killed in action, storming an enemy naval camp in Cilicia, where Megabyxos, the conqueror of Egypt, was again methodically preparing a counter-stroke. Anaxikrates may well have been killed in a raid intended to interfere with the "build-up"; but the muddled narrative of Diodoros of

Sicily contains more rhetoric than information. Meanwhile Kimon lay in his tent before Kition, sick of a fever and troubled, like Douglas in the ballad, by omens and evil dreams:

> "But I hae dreamed a weary dream
> Beyond the isle of Skye;
> I saw a dead man win a fight
> And I think that man was I."

Then the blow fell; as in the Ionian revolt fifty years before, the Persians, though outmatched at sea, managed to run troops across from Cilicia, probably waiting for a north wind, which would make it dangerous for Greek ships to linger off the rocky north coast and a slow business to beat up from the south. Kimon from his bed gave the orders for the Greek counter-operation. Breaking off the siege of Kition, his army marched across the island, while his fleet bore up to the northward round its eastern end. He seems already to have called in his Egyptian squadron. In the double battle of the Cypriote Salamis they once more defeated Persians and Phœnicians by land and sea; but the victory gained the expedition nothing more than an unmolested retreat. The enemy forces were still in being, and could be reinforced more easily than the invaders; and, most distressingly, many Cypriotes seem to have been rallying to the Persian side. Kimon's staff embarked their land forces and sailed for home; and the allies did not know till many days later that the cabin on the flag-ship now held only the dust of the great admiral.

So passed Kimon.

To Pericles and the peace party this was an opportunity not to be missed. The King of Persia had been shown that Athens and the League were still formidable; and, on the other hand, the forty thousand young men who served on the expedition had found that, even under Kimon, it was not the expected picnic, nor had the Egyptian disaster been merely an inexplicable fluke.

Both sides were ready for peace. The veteran Kallias

was sent to Susa, and in 449, on terms of which neither side was very proud at the time, the Persian War was officially brought to an end. The Great King undertook not to send warships into the Sea of Marmara or the Ægean, and western Asia Minor seems to have been demilitarised by both sides; but Athens abandoned her allies in Cyprus and Egypt, whom the Persians proceeded to wear down at their leisure. It was not, it seems, till the next century that Athens felt inclined to inscribe a version of the "glorious" Peace of Kallias on stone by way of contrast with the far more ignominious peace then made by Sparta.[3]

[3] The inscription was in the Ionic alphabet, which was not in official use at Athens until 403. This led the "debunking" historian Theopompos to deny that Athens ever imposed such a peace at all; and some moderns have followed him. It is true that the sketch in Thucydides' Introduction omits all mention of the Peace, as it omits many other things; but in Thucydides' narrative proper we find that the negotiations of 411 between Athens and Persia break down precisely on the questions of Athens' *permitting* the king to bring warships into the Ægean, and ceding Ionia. This is surely conclusive evidence that there was a treaty. As to why the published text which Theopompos saw was in Ionic, one suggestion is given above; there are other possibilities.

See Wade-Gery, *The Peace of Kallias* (cf. Note on Books.)

Chapter 7

The Years of Crisis (2)

THE PEACE OF KALLIAS, following on the truce with
Sparta, left Athens without a war on her hands, supreme
in every part of the Ægean, in the Corinthian Gulf, and
on the Greek mainland from Megara to Thermopylæ.
Embassies came even from Rhegion (Reggio, on the
Sicilian straits) and from Leontinoi, south of Mount Etna,
both old colonies of Chalkis, asking for Athenian protection against big and aggressive Dorian Syracuse. Pericles
was not altogether pleased. No sooner had he got Athens
clear of one commitment than another turned up. He saw
clearly by now that the most dangerous trait of the Assembly was over-confidence; if not treated to a good deal
of cold water, they would end by straining the city's
elastic, but not unlimited, strength to breaking-point. But
the Assembly was delighted, and voted friendship and
alliance "for ever" with both cities.

Meanwhile Athens was confronted with the perhaps
unforeseen fact that peace has her problems no less difficult than those of war; especially those of demobilisation.
What was to be done with all those thousands of citizens
who in the past thirty years had lived, as soldiers and
sailors, largely on the contributions of the Empire?

This raised the further question, what should happen
about these contributions, now that the Persian War had
been wound up? To the allies it was quite plain what
ought to happen. The covenant of the League, as Wade-
Gery puts it, lasted "till the iron swam," but the cities
that found ships for the fleet found them in war-time only.
Correspondingly, in peace-time the money paid by most
members in lieu of ships, being a war contribution, should

not be levied. There is in fact a Tribute-list missing from about this time among the surviving records of the Delian League; and in view of the number of fragments which do survive from the great marble slab, on which these lists were originally published, it is rather unlikely that a whole list has perished without trace. Meritt and Wade-Gery conclude that, in fact, in the first year of peace no tribute was paid.

The cessation of war and of war contributions confronted Athens with a formidable problem of unemployment; the same problem that confronted Rome some centuries later. Probably Pericles, for all his intelligence, had not foreseen it; it has been very rare indeed in history for statesmen to foresee an entirely new type of economic situation before it has arisen. Normally after a Greek summer war, the citizen soldiers and sailors went thankfully back to their farms or trades, and the problem did not arise. Even the wars of the Delian League had for the most part been seasonal. Almost every sailor in Piræus must therefore have had a home of his own, at least in the sense of a place where he went in the winter; so the problem was not quite like a modern problem of resettlement. But never before in Greece had so many men been out on service every summer for so many years on end; and never before had there been concentrated in one place so large a population as now in Athens and Piræus (especially Piræus, with its large immigrant element) divorced from the land.

The first year of peace, with the task of feeding some twenty thousand sailors who would "normally" have been abroad for the summer, must have brought the problem home to everybody. The poor, his supporters, looked to their great leader Pericles to produce a plan for them.

Pericles did not fail; nor indeed would it have taken a Pericles to devise the solution or palliative: a great programme of public works. The temples on the Acropolis had been lying waste ever since the Persians burnt them thirty-two years before. Some foundations had been laid, under Kimon; but that was before Athens had fought Persia and the Peloponnesians both at once. Since then little had been done.

Work on the site for a great new national temple was probably put in hand at once. At the same time Pericles proposed, and the Assembly charged him to carry out, the construction of a new "middle" long wall from Athens to Piræus, strengthening the linked fortress—little necessary as it might seem in the heyday of Athenian sea-power —by protecting the rear of the original Piræus wall against a sea-borne raid, such as the Spartan Brasidas once attempted, on Phaleron Bay. Here, also, preliminaries took some time. The first preserved to us of many gibes at Pericles in the topical comedies, which people were just beginning to preserve in book form, comes from Kratinos, a tough old Tory:

"Pericles has been building it with words since long ago,
But as for doing anything, there isn't much to show."

One seems to have heard his remark made in other contexts.

At the same time Piræus was being equipped with worthy public buildings; its pillared Corn Exchange facing the Great Harbour, and the Deigma, or Mart, where merchants displayed their samples were beautiful as well as useful; and the new town-centre was not allowed to grow up anyhow, like the little old island towns, but laid out systematically with broad main streets by the first town-planner in history, a young political theorist, Hippodamos of Miletos.

But Pericles did not stop there. To crown the Acropolis with a temple worthy of Athens was for him the fulfilment of an ideal, and not only a means to a "full employment policy"; but at the same time he took a step that showed friend and foe how he dreamed of Athens as nothing less than the capital of Greece. On his motion, the Assembly invited all the states of Greece and the Ægean to send delegates to a conference at Athens, to consult "about [the restoration of] the temples of Greece burnt by the barbarians; and about the sacrifices owed to the Gods in payment of the vows which we made when fighting the barbarians; and about the sea, that all men may sail it in security and peace."

These were unexceptionable words; but it must have been plain to all that the only important temples burnt by the Persians, except in Ionia, had been the temples of Athens, and that the project of a conference on the freedom and security of the seas amounted to an invitation to all to recognise the Athenian navy as a pan-Hellenic institution. The envoys sent to the Peloponnese met with a blunt refusal, and Sparta also used her influence to oppose the project elsewhere. The proposed conference never took place.

It is difficult to imagine that Pericles expected any other result; but he had put out his manifesto. He had put forward the theses that the restoration of the Athenian temples was an obligation to all Greece, and that the Athenian navy, by driving the Persians from the Ægean and suppressing piracy, was performing a common Hellenic service. On this moral basis he now required the cities of the Delian League to continue to pay their contributions in time of peace.

The formal step was taken by Kleinias: almost certainly the son of that Alkibiades who had fought with Kleisthenes, the husband of Pericles' kinswoman Deinomache, and the father of an infant Alkibiades, who was to be famous in his day. Kleinias proposed a decree, which is still extant, instructing "the Council [at Athens], the governments of the Cities and the [Athenian] Inspectors to take measures for the annual collection of the tribute and its delivery to Athens." The Council is to note cases of default or negligence and refer them to the Law Courts "without delay." Envoys are to be sent out round the empire to acquaint "the Cities" with the Athenian Assembly's decision. Among further details, every city is also to send a panoply of arms and a cow for sacrifice, to the grand quadriennial festival at Athens, the Great Panathenaia. The Athenian Empire was taking its final shape.

So in the civil year 448-447 the collection of tribute

recommenced; but not without friction, as is shown by the quota-list for the year. The last list (No. 5, for 450-449) had had room for 175 to 180 names of cities. The new list (No. 7) which is almost complete, contains 146 names, with room in the destroyed portion for not more than four more; i.e. twenty-five or thirty cities which paid in 450 defaulted altogether in the year 448. What is still more significant is the proportion of the richer and more powerful cities among those absent. The missing names include Miletos, Ephesos, Kyzikos, and Aigina; Lampsakos made a token payment, under 10 per cent of her assessment; Thasos, Byzantion, and the rich Thracian coast cities of Ainos and Abdera paid in part only. These nine cities with Perinthos (also on the Sea of Marmara), which perhaps paid nothing, normally produced over a quarter of the whole tribute of the League.

Sparta also was being difficult. Pericles had, no doubt, meant to use the Five Year Truce in order to negotiate a more lasting settlement; he could make soundings all the more easily and quietly from the fact that he knew the Spartan King Archidamos quite well; there was a family friendship between their houses. But the Spartan Assembly (the "Peers," who elected the annual executive, the five Ephors) were bellicose—all the more so with Kimon gone and his policy torn up. They were still bound by truce to Athens—but, sailing as near the wind as possible, in 448 they sent a force across the Corinthian Gulf, for the first time since Tanagra, to vindicate the independence of Delphi against the Phokians, Athens' allies, in whose territory it lay.

Pericles, anxious for peace though he was, had no doubt about how to deal with such a provocation. He merely waited until the Spartans had gone home, and then with an adequate force marched on Delphi and put the administration of the sanctuary back into the hands of the Phokians. The Spartans had left a record of their passage: an inscription granting precedence to the Spartan liberators in consulting the oracle (for which there was often so long a queue that one might have to wait in an inn for weeks). The inscription had been cut by the Delphians on the forehead of the great bronze wolf (the sacred beast of Apollo) that stood before the Temple. Pericles got a similar decree passed in favour of Athens, and inscribed on the right flank of the same wolf.

At the same time Athens renewed her oaths of friendship and alliance with the Phokians. That rough highland confederacy, for all its debt of gratitude to Athens, does not seem to have felt any devoted affection for its strange, revolutionary, democratic protectors.

There were ominous rumblings in Boiotia, too. The weak democracy at Thebes had governed badly, and was tottering to its fall. Across the narrow seas, Euboia was seething with discontent. Several cities there seem to have commuted ships for a money payment no longer ago than 450, and now found that tribute, unlike a contingent, was expected in peace-time. The mountains of northern Greece, beyond Athens' reach, were full of angry anti-Athenian exiles, biding their time. Altogether, Pericles seems to have come back from Delphi with grave doubts whether, in the event of any serious trouble, the mainland position could be held.

There was violent opposition to Pericles also at home. The conservatives chose as their new leader Thoukydides, son of Pindar's old friend the famous wrestling-trainer Melesias, and a connection, probably brother-in-law, of Kimon. The plans for the great new Temple (selection of artists, grants of money, etc.) were going through the Assembly this year (work started in earnest in 447), and the conservatives fought them line by line. Their ground of principle was the strong one that Athens had no right to apply the money, voted by the Allies for the war against Persia, to purely Athenian purposes. Their ground of interest was that they were "little Athenians," dreaming of the good old days, of an Athens of noblemen and farmers, before this great wen of a seaport arose and spread. Kimon had been an imperialist; but that was when Athens was still fighting Persia. Also it was the well-to-do classes in the Empire, the Athenian conservatives' "opposite numbers," who paid the bulk of the tribute, and who, if anyone could, might help to check the march of urban democracy.

Thoukydides, having less personal prestige than Kimon, did his best to compensate for the lack by more systematic party management than had yet been seen in the Assembly. His supporters—mostly people who could afford to give their time—were systematically "whipped up," and were instructed to sit together, to show their numerical strength and still more their social rank. Social prestige still counted for a good deal at Athens. No doubt they also began to use regular cheer-leaders. But in a full "house" they succeeded rather in showing their numerical weakness, and Pericles promptly underlined it by dubbing them "the Few," which carried a nasty connotation of "the would-be oligarchs."

It is not recorded that Thoukydides ever succeeded in carrying an important motion against Pericles and the democrats, but he made Pericles fight hard. Echoes of the debate on financing the Parthenon find their way down the centuries into Plutarch's *Pericles*. "The name of Athens," declaimed the conservatives, "has been brought into dishonour and reproach by our transfer of the common funds of Greece to Athens from Delos; and now we are deprived of our best excuse for doing this—the need for security against the barbarians—by Pericles. Greece feels herself the victim of oppression and tyranny when she sees us using the money, forcibly levied for purposes of war, on the gilding and glorifying of our city, and Athens decking herself like a vain woman with precious stones and statues and thousand-talent temples. . . ."

Pericles' reply was pitched in a lower key. "He expounded to the people," we are told (it is symbolic of the position that he was now reaching that the word used is "teach"—the word reserved nowadays by minor communist writers for Marx, Engels, Lenin, and Stalin), "that they had no obligation to give any account of expenditure to the allies, so long as they fought for them" and kept off the barbarians from "these allies, who do not produce so much as one horse, one ship, or one man-at-arms, but simply money. Money is the property not of those who pay it but of those who receive it, so long as they perform the service for which they are paid. Athens has every right, once she has equipped herself adequately with weapons of war, to employ her wealth on objects like these: objects that when acccomplished will be a glory for ever, while during their accomplishment they will be a source of prosperity, creating a demand for every kind of labour, stimulating every craft and setting every hand in motion, bringing almost the whole city into state employment, adorning itself and feeding itself both at once."

The majority rallied to Pericles, and work went forward; but things had not yet gone far on the Acropolis, when news came in, in autumn 447, that an armed insurrection had broken out in western Boiotia.

In the debate that followed, or in the little that we know of it, Thoukydides and the conservatives do not appear. Old-fashioned patriotism perhaps, and political tactics certainly, forbade that they should come out openly as anti-imperialists in such a crisis. The chief argument was between Pericles, urging caution, and Tolmides, the probably younger, certainly more impetuous, imperialist general.

The situation was that a band of anti-Athenian exiles, Boiotians, Lokrians, and Euboians, all acting together, had seized the remotest cities of Boiotia, Orchomenos, and Chaironeia. Tolmides was all for immediate, decisive military action to crush the revolt before it had time to spread. With 1,000 Athenian armoured infantry and the local allies, he was sure it could be done.

Pericles, the statesman, took a far graver view of the rising and thought Tolmides' project perilous. He was for waiting—presumably to combine political action with military operations on a larger and more deliberate scale. But he was defeated—the last defeat of Pericles in the Assembly on a major issue for a long time. His last word in the debate was: "If you will not obey Pericles, at least you will not be wrong in heeding that surest of all counsellors, Time." At that moment people thought him overcautious; but later the saying was remembered.

What does not appear is why Tolmides did not at least take a larger force. It was "winter," that is to say late autumn, with snow beginning to fall on the high mountains, and rain in the lowlands; a season at which campaigning was extremely unpopular with Greek citizen troops. But a thousand armoured men was very few. It is not unlikely that a considerable number of Athenian troops was still scattered over the Empire, seeing to the collecting of tribute under Kleinias' decree.

Tolmides, however, called for volunteers, and got them without difficulty—mostly adventurous young men of the land-owning classes. Kleinias was one of the senior men among them, perhaps a general. There were also allied contingents, probably from the faithful Plataia and from the other Boiotian cities in alliance with Athens. Just how unreliable, by now, local allies were, Tolmides did not appreciate.

Tolmides and his men took Chaironeia and sold their prisoners as slaves, a severe measure of reprisal; but Orchomenos, on its long steep-sided spur with the castle at its top, was too much for him either to blockade or storm. He garrisoned Chaironeia and started to lead his army home, between Lake Kopaïs and Mount Helikon.

Mount Helikon is a spreading, forested region, much cloven, owing to the lie of the geological strata, by parallel glens running east and west; an insidious mountain, offering possibilities of concealed movement that have repeatedly been found useful by modern guerillas. By such a route the exiles and their local supporters now got ahead of Tolmides and lay in wait for him at Koroneia, where a south-to-north valley opens into the plain. Some local shepherd or goatherd could have warned Tolmides of his danger; but Athens had taken no trouble to cultivate the people among her continental allies. She now paid the penalty. On the road from Lebadeia to Haliartos, the exiles fell upon Tolmides' marching columns. The Athenian "allies" leave no mark in history—probably they dissolved without striking a blow. Tolmides, Kleinias, and many others fell fighting, and more than half the

Athenians, broken and hemmed in, were forced to surrender.

The Boiotian nationalists thus made an invaluable haul of well-born Athenian hostages; and to secure their release, the Assembly abandoned all its claims to suzerainty in Boiotia. Every city except Plataia broke off its alliance with Athens, and Thebes resumed her normal position as "managing director" in the Boiotian League. Constitutions were revised in an oligarchic sense—in Athenian parlance, "the people were enslaved"; and no more was heard of democracy in Boiotia so long as Athens remained the leading power in Greece.

Pericles might at least hope, however, to have gained Boiotia's benevolent neutrality instead of her unwilling submission; and this hope, for a time, was justified. It was well for Athens; for the Five Years' Truce with Sparta was coming to an end, and without even waiting for the Spartans to march, the movement of rebellion now spread to Euboia.

Tribute List No. 9 shows that the Euboians paid their quotas in the spring of 446; the rebellion probably followed as soon as the islanders had thus got rid of the armed tribute-collecting expeditions, which Athens often sent out where difficulties were expected.

The protagonist of vigorous action this time was Pericles himself. Euboia was no mainland ally but an essential part of the Delian League. A strong force under Pericles was ordered to Euboia, while three regiments under Andokides covered Megara, holding the passes of Geraneia against any threat from the Peloponnese. But scarcely had Pericles crossed the water when he was recalled by far worse news. The Peloponnesians were marching, and Megara had revolted with help from Corinth, Epidauros, and Sikyon, massacring her Athenian garrison, and cutting communications with Athens in the rear of Andokides' army.

With great difficulty and not without fighting, Andokides' three regiments made their way back: "pulling in" first to Pagai on the west coast, where they left a garrison, and then, by mule-tracks and sheep-tracks, to Aigosthena on the extreme northeast corner of the gulf, and probably over the high shoulder of Kithairon to Plataia. Thence through Boiotia they made their way back to Athens. Their guide in this adventure was one Pythion, a Megarian wood-cutter and evidently a stout democrat, who killed seven men with his own hand and "brought honour to Andokides with two thousand men." He lived the rest of his life at Athens, where his pleasantly illiterate epitaph (perhaps his own composition) gives us these details of his and Andokides' adventures.

Among those who took part in this adventure was, in all probability, Socrates, as a twenty-four-year-old soldier in the Antiochis Regiment.

The united army stood before Athens, but it was terribly outnumbered by the great masses of spearmen who now poured into Attica. It was 507 over again: the Peloponnesians in front and a hostile Euboia unopposed in the rear. True, Boiotia was neutral now; but, on the other hand, there was no hope this time of a friendly Corinth to take the lead in upsetting Sparta's designs. . . . And yet to everybody's amazement exactly the same thing happened again. The Peloponnesian army reached Eleusis and came on almost to the Aigaleos Ridge; and there they halted and, without fighting, turned about and went home.

What had happened behind the scenes was, of course, "most secret"; but few people had any doubt about it, least of all the government of Sparta. The young king Pleistoanax, who had been in titular command of the expedition, was brought to trial on his return (such things could be done at Sparta), and sentenced to a heavy fine, and went into exile. Simultaneously his chief of staff, the great soldier Kleandridas, fled for fear of arrest. The Spartans tried him in his absence and condemned him to death. He was the father of that Gylippos who was thirty years later to overthrow the Athenians in Sicily, and at last to be condemned for corruption in his turn.

Pericles kept his own counsel; besides, he was busy. With fifty ships and 5,000 armoured men—leaving fully half the first-line army this time to guard against other threats—he crossed again to Euboia and, in probably his most brilliant campaign, crushed the rebellion in one summer. A new *clêrûchy* of 1,000 families was planted at Oreos in the territory of Hestiaia, in the north of the island, through which Athens could control communications between Euboia and the northern mainland; and the whole population of Hestiaia was driven out. This was justified by Pericles as reprisal, because during the rebellion they had massacred the crew of an Athenian ship.

The other Euboian cities were treated gently. Their tribute was not raised, and they kept control of their internal affairs, Athens retaining, as was now usual, certain overriding powers, especially the function of the Athenian juries as a court of appeal. The Euboians enjoyed even the right of intermarriage with Athenians. But it was too late. For all the liberality of the settlement—a Periclean settlement—Athens never hereafter ceased to feel nervous about Euboia. Thirty-five years later, in Athens' dark hour, the islanders took the first opportunity to revolt successfully.

We have the text of the Decree providing for the ratification of the treaty with Chalkis. The people of Chalkis are secured against the fate of Hestiaia; but they formally swear allegiance to the People of Athens, alone. We have travelled a long way since Erythrai swore allegiance to the People of Athens and the Allies.

It remained to settle with Sparta. That Athens should agree to concessions with her main forces undefeated is unparalleled in Athenian history. Not to make concessions, at this juncture, would have been to invite disaster; yet for the fact that on this occasion they were made, credit is probably due to Pericles. Andokides and the veteran Kallias, now performing his last service to Athens, were among the envoys sent to Sparta; and in that winter, 446-445, a thirty years' peace was at last signed. Athens gave up Nisaia and Pagai, the ports of Megara, and withdrew from the Peloponnese, abandoning Troizen and Achaia, though not her *entente* with Argos; but she kept her Ægean empire, including Aigina subject to some stipulations about "autonomy" (internal home rule). She also kept Naupaktos.

It was a triumph for Periclean policy—a triumph, not least, over the Athenian Assembly—for the policy of holding fast to the maritime Empire, eschewing risky adventures, and conserving above all the precious resources of Athenian manpower.

At the end of that year Pericles had an item in his accounts which he did not wish to discuss. In the end he wrote down:

"To necessary expenditure: 10 Talents"

and left it at that. The people would scarcely have taken such treatment from anyone else; but they took it from Pericles. Indeed, according to one account, a "secret vote" became after this, while Pericles lived, a regular item. "Necessary expenditure" became a standard "quotation" at Athens, and remained a popular joke for at least forty years.

It would scarcely have done to write down: "To bribery of one Spartan King and his Chief-of-Staff"; but Pericles certainly appears to have bought them cheap. What he had probably done, in fact, was to persuade them in earnest that he intended to sue for peace, offering concessions; which was true. He could then offer his ten talents as a secret *douceur* for calling off their army without further devastation. What the two Spartans had not appreciated was that, in the time thus gained, Pericles could secure the one vital point, Euboia. As Pericles said of one of his secret payments: "What I bought was not peace, but time."

So Pericles had his peace, with the tribute. Now there would be time and money for that great efflorescence of Athenian building, sculpture, and music that was nearest his heart.

The year 445 is a notable date in history; for the Thirty Years' Peace (though it lasted less than fifteen) gave respite in which those buildings were completed, which spring to the mind's eye of every man who hears the name of Athens.

It was not that the treaty was greeted anywhere with acclamation at the time. A trying war had ended in a compromise peace. There was relief, perhaps, but few cities were without some cause for dissatisfaction; many had cause for shame. At Sparta, victory had been marred by a shocking scandal and bought by the sacrifice of allies. Corinth had to acquiesce in the presence of Athenian allies at Naupaktos, on her main trade route. Euboia and Aigina were back under the yoke. For Athens, it was defeat, though—thanks to Pericles—not disaster. The tough bargaining of Kallias and Andokides had kept Aigina and Naupaktos, though not Troizen and Achaia. Well, thought some people, these places would be a good springboard for another time. If Athenian sea-power could penetrate the west as Athenian trade had long been doing, the Peloponnese might be caught in a nut-cracker grip. Some good modern authorities believe that Pericles was among these, and that the "Athens-Sparta dualism" which the new treaty consecrated was anathema to him; but for this the present writer can see little evidence. It is not often that a politician—even a Pericles—can foresee the long-term consequences of his acts, as they can be seen long after. We have no evidence that Pericles dreamed of a political unification of Greece—an idea that would have seemed monstrous to most of his contemporaries. The primacy of Athens *in* Greece was something quite different; no dream, but already a reality. As to the *Drang nach Westen,* Plutarch's evidence, for what it is worth, is that Pericles viewed it without enthusiasm as offering awkward commitments and potential dangers. What really and most deeply interested him, there is ample evidence, was the building programme.

Among the few groups with real cause for enthusiasm over this dénouement were the Theban aristocrats, who had recovered control in their own city and the leadership in Boiotia. We have a poem by a Theban, the now aged Pindar, for a victory won in 446 by a boy wrestler of Aigina. In it he salutes for the last time the island city that he had hymned so often and loved so well. Let others deal in power and violence, he says, like the giants that Athene tamed of old (like Athens, he seems to hint). In Aigina there is justice and righteousness, the honour of ancient heroes, and the "gleam from heaven" that sheds a radiance of peace over the shortness and frailty of human happiness. There is even the hope of freedom. (Did not a clause in the Treaty guarantee Aigina home-rule? But, alas, the reality was to be a sad disappointment after the poet's hope.) The whole poem—the Eighth Pythian Ode—is like a swan-song of the older Greece, the world, as Wade-Gery says, which Athens meant to break and build again; but which, as it was, was broken and remained so.

Nor was Athens herself unscathed. Once more, as in the Egyptian disaster, though on a less disastrous scale, something irreplaceable had perished with Tolmides and Kleinias and their young men. The defeat of Tolmides was a blow to the centre party, that "green earth school" among the imperialists, whose lineage went back to Kimon and Aristeides. With the loss of the land empire, the predominant importance of the navy was accentuated; and from this time forth, the quality and morale of the Athenian army slightly but definitely declined. All the more stark was the antithesis between the radical imperialists—"the nautical rabble" as the conservatives called them—and the anti-imperialists under Thoukydides. Some more of the year had gone, in Pericles' metaphor. What remains is the garnering, under Pericles himself, of a wonderful harvest; but no second spring.

PART III
PERICLEAN ATHENS

Chapter 8

The Supremacy of Pericles

THE EVENTS of 446 finally raised Pericles to a position of honour and trust in Athens such as no other statesman was ever to enjoy; but the effect was not felt immediately. The immediate sequel to the peace of 445 was a reaction, in both the political and psychological sense of the word. In 444 Pericles, for the last time in his life, was not elected general. Thoukydides, the son of Melesias (to judge by a muddled passage from a biography of his namesake the historian), probably was.

One day during the struggle with Thoukydides, a "portent," i.e. a monstrosity, was brought into Pericles' town house from one of his farms. It was a ram, with one eye in the centre of its forehead and one horn. Lampon the seer (it is of interest to find that the "rationalist" Pericles had a seer in his entourage) prophesied: This portended that the two powers in the state would shortly be reduced to one, the prophet's patron. But the scientist Anaxagoras sawed the beast's skull in two, and demonstrated that the phenomenon was due to natural causes, being incidental to a deformation of the cranium. At the moment, says Plutarch, Anaxagoras was held to have scored; but later people remembered Lampon's saying. Pericles, however, was shortly to lose the company of both these old associates.

It was customary at Athens to use the law courts as a field of political operations, and just as Ephialtes and Pericles had prosecuted Areopagites as part of the "softening-up" process before their assault on that Council, so now and later Pericles' rivals or ill-wishers, finding the great man's own position impregnable, tried to weaken it—to weaken Pericles' credit with the multitude, that is —by gaining decisions against his friends. There was nothing *necessarily* mean and malicious about the process,

115

any more than about all politics. If one was a friend of a prominent politician, one had to expect that sort of thing, and to watch one's step accordingly.

Thoukydides' partisans attacked both in the law courts and by way of *ostrakismós*. In the first three years of the peace there were probably at least two *ostrakismói* if not three. Pericles' old mentor Damon is said to have succumbed, and an *ostrakon* with his name, from a vase painted after 450, dates the event to these years. A considerable bunch of sherds has also turned up against Kleïppides of Acharnai, one of the generals left by Pericles at his death fifteen years later; and scattered votes appear against others of the group, such as Andokides and Teisandros, son of Epilykos, who, though probably a Philaïd like Thoukydides himself, chose to betroth his daughters to the sons of Andokides and Pericles.

Probably at the same time old Anaxagoras was prosecuted for irreligion. Since the fall of the great meteorite at the Goat Rivers in 462, he had been evolving startling views on the nature of the heavenly bodies, finally declaring the conclusion that the sun was "a mass of incandescent stone, probably larger than the whole of the Peloponnese." Such views might be all very well in Ionia; but Athens—contrary to most modern belief—was a different matter. Some intellectual (mostly aristocratic) circles might indulge in daring speculations; but ordinary Athenian opinion was conventional, religious, and, when roused, intolerant. Even so, public opinion would probably *not* have been roused against Anaxagoras, had not some influential people been anxious to discredit Pericles by showing the kind of company he kept. A well-known oracle-monger named Diopeithes, with a crippled hand, venomous, fanatical, unbalanced, but not on that account any less convincing as a "holy man," carried a decree in the Assembly making "those who do not believe in the Gods, or who teach doctrines concerning the heavenly bodies," liable to impeachment before the Assembly itself. Thoukydides, according to one story, then led the attack on Anaxagoras, bringing in among other subsidiary charges—for relevance to the case was no object in an Athenian trial—that of being pro-Persian, a "collaborator." The charge is credible enough; ages ago, in his home in Klazomenai, he had lived under the Persians, and he was clearly an "unattached," unpolitical, unworldly intellectual—no violent nationalist or "underground" worker. Pericles was constrained to smuggle his old friend away, either before trial or from prison after condemnation; such things could be done in Athens, and Thoukydides did not really want the elderly scientist put to death, as those convicted of impiety could be. Anaxagoras retired to the rich Ionian colony of Lampsakos on the Dardanelles, where he became a local celebrity and taught philosophy till his death in 428. His last request, in reply to an enquiry from the city authorities, what form of memorial he would like, was that the anniversary of his death might be kept in perpetuity as a holiday for schoolchildren.

But Thoukydides entirely failed to eliminate Pericles himself. No serious charge would lie against him, and at the *ostrakophoriai* it seems that, even in an anti-radical mood, the people turned aside to vote against Damon, Andokides, Teisandros, anyone but the great liberal leader. Out of all the many hundreds of *ostraka* known, chiefly from the American excavations, it was not till 1940 that a single example turned up bearing Pericles' name. It is not surprising to find that it was inscribed by an old-fashioned citizen, in a style of writing commoner in the 'sixties or 'seventies. Pericles hit back with a prosecution of a friend of Thoukydides named Pyrilampes, before the Areopagus, for murder—a *crime passionel*; but the young man was successfully defended by Thoukydides himself.

The chief events of these years in ordinary politics had to do with the post-war problems of food and resettlement. In 445 an Egyptian prince, Psammetichos, son of the ill-fated Inaros, who was still holding out in the Delta, sent Athens a "bakshish" of 30,000 bushels of wheat; and the arrangements for distributing this among the poorer citizens led to an appalling crop of disputed-citizenship cases under the Act of 451. Some thousands of people, who under Pericles' act were not qualified, were, it appears, still registered in the various wards. The impending distribution of corn gave the Assembly an immediate concrete reason for querying doubtful claims. A scrutiny of the registers was ordered, and out of 19,000 cases (perhaps the total number of adult males of the Labourer class claiming citizenship in the urban wards) nearly 5,000 are said to have been struck off. The whole episode is an ominous reminder of the widening gulf between Athenian citizens and other subjects of the empire.

In the same year Athens made a new move in the west; a measure offering some consolation to "displaced persons" who could no longer hope for Athenian citizenship. After the embassies from Egesta, Rhegion, and Leontinoi, a group of men from Sybaris had appeared in Athens begging for Athenian help to re-establish their city. Sybaris was that once fabulously wealthy city in south Italy, which under a revolutionary democracy had been wiped off the map by the sister-city of Kroton, under a puritan aristocracy—that strange "rule of the saints" organised by the followers of Pythagoras. That was fifty-seven years before, and since then the surviving Sybarites had lived obscurely at their daughter-colonies across the "instep" of Italy, on the west coast. But the Pythagorean governments at Kroton and in the neighbouring states had now fallen in a series of bloody popular revolutions, and Sybaris began to raise her head again.

The Assembly accepted the invitation and sent ten ships with colonists. Among them was Herodotos, the historian and traveller, who had settled at Athens too late to gain citizenship. Their leaders were two prophets, Lampon and Xenokritos; they duly consulted the Delphic Oracle, and received a suitably cryptic answer about where to settle, which they had no difficulty in interpreting to the general satisfaction. Athens also invited colonists from the Empire and from mainland Greece—a gesture of goodwill towards late enemies, which both Thoukydides and Pericles must surely have approved. The colony had its growing-pains, especially when the Sybarites claimed privileges as compared with the new-comers, and were driven out by them; but ultimately, at the adjacent site of Thouria, a new city arose, laid out in the modern style by Hippodamos, the town-planner of Piræus, with broad main thoroughfares crossing at right angles. It suffered some reverses in a war with the Dorians of Taras (Tarentum, Taranto), the most powerful state in south Italy since the decline of Kroton, but presently found a useful general in Kleandridas the Spartan, who had been unemployed since 446 and presumably living on his bribes.

Thoukydides also (probably as general in 444) sailed out to take a hand in the proceedings; but the expedition was fatal to him. He quarrelled with Xenokritos, who followed him back to Athens and prosecuted him when they arrived, what for does not appear; but Pericles seized the opportunity for a counter-attack; another *ostrakophoria* was held in spring, 443, and Thoukydides was banished. With his departure the effective resistance of the conservative party broke up. Its extremists resorted to dreams of treason; some of its members (young Pyrilampes, for example) were reconciled to Pericles; and Pericles emerged as the one indubitable "national" leader of Athens. He never had another serious political rival.

To this final period belong nearly all the contemporary anecdotes and impressions of Pericles, which Plutarch, with his neglect of chronology, imagines to be equally applicable to any time since 469. He was now obviously, as well as really, the most important man not only in Athens but in the Mediterranean world. Plain men throughout Greece, and governments from Persia to Carthage, wanted to know about him. Anecdotes, quotations from his speeches, anything that might shed a light on his personality was avidly repeated. Soon after his death details about him were even circulating in books, in the new prose literature for general consumption; books such as that of Stesimbrotos the Thasian, scurrilous and very hostile, and the *Memoirs* of the tragedian Ion of Chios, as well as the admiring sketch in the history of Thucydides. There are also the caricaturing hits at him from Athenian comedies, some light-hearted, some really hostile, the only extant words about him which were written down, as we have them, in his lifetime. For his later years, and for them only, therefore, Pericles' private as well as his public life is fairly well documented.

To these years, then, belongs that picture of the "Olympian" Pericles which we owe to Plutarch; Pericles who "knew only the streets between his home and the government offices" (or the city and Parliament Hill), who "never went to parties," and who found out a new way of dealing with his property, so as to be freed from a great landowner's usual preoccupations.

What Pericles did about this was to sell the produce of his land wholesale, year by year, and send his steward out to buy his town household's daily food, wine, oil, etcetera, retail in the market. Inevitably he lost money on the transaction, but he saved immensely in time; and he lost much less than he would have if he had simply relied on his estates for maintenance, in the traditional manner, without giving them personal attention. (As a Greek proverb said, the best food for cattle is the master's eye.) It seems likely that he did this annual wholesale selling *in advance*. Responsibility for looking after the corn, the vines, and the olive crops thus devolved on the buyers; the system amounted to letting out the various fields on annual tenancies. Pericles thus transferred his whole domestic economy on to a money basis; still a novelty, it appears, among the land-owning families. Careful accounts were kept (necessarily, when supplies were being bought retail); and the whole system was looked after by the steward Euangelos, who had grown up under Pericles to his present position of responsibility.

Euangelos was evidently a "treasure," but in other quarters this way of running a household was far from popular. In fact, it really bore rather hardly on Pericles' sons, especially on Xanthippos, the elder, who some time in the 'thirties married, as above-mentioned, an aristocratic young lady, the daughter of Teisandros. She found it quite incredible that while her two sisters, who were married to the sons of Andokides and of the Leagros who was killed in Thrace, had everything "off the estate" with-

out stint, the son of Pericles was kept on a strict and (to
the young people's minds) parsimonious allowance in
money. Glaukon, the son of Leagros, of course, had his
family estate as his own; but old Andokides was alive,
and *he* did not keep his son short like that. Thus the
young woman nagged, and Xanthippos, already not on
good terms with his father, grew more disgruntled still.

A solution, one would have thought, might have been
that the sons, with Euangelos to help them, should run the
estates; but this Pericles never seems to have contem-
plated. He did not trust his sons, and was disappointed
in them, especially in Xanthippos. It was a nemesis on
him for past neglect; and yet the fault was not wholly
Pericles' own, but largely that—as usual—of a society in
transition. Athenian fathers never had made much fuss of
their sons, and so long as society was divided only into
large and small farmers, it had not mattered very much;
the boys grew up on the estate, in daily unsentimental
contact with father, until they were old enough to be useful. But when father's work was that of a fifth-century
general, the result—with no schools but elementary day-
schools—was neglect. Certainly, every "young gentleman"
had an attendant, the *paidagôgos,* usually some decent,
elderly, family slave, who was getting past other work.
Devotedly loyal (to judge by the *paidagôgoi* in the plays)
these old men often were; but for keeping the "young
master" out of mischief, and even more for inculcating
any reasoned code of ethics, they were of course useless.

Social usage, too, was responsible for those grim,
"duty" marriages, felt to be cruel even in Athens itself, in
which a girl left without brothers was married off to her
nearest male relative to perpetuate her father's family, at
the cost of two divorces if necessary. Pericles, indeed, in
liberal fashion, had let his wife go where she would when
she had borne him two sons; but even that had not been
good for the boys; it merely meant that they lacked not
only a father's but a mother's personal attention. Victims
of neglect, Xanthippos and Paralos, though not without
intelligent interests, drifted into bad company, and were
never anything to their father but an additional worry.

Pericles' "Olympian" outlook had led him to ideas in advance of his age in some matters, but not in the most fundamental of all.

Pericles' household contained two other young hopefuls besides his own sons. Kleinias, the son of Alkibiades, killed in action in 447, had left two boys, called respectively after his father and himself; and they fell under the joint guardianship of their cousins, Pericles and his brother. Ariphron being a complete nonentity, the greater part of the burden fell upon Pericles, or rather upon Pericles' domestic staff; and no small burden it proved.

The young Alkibiades, beautiful, lively, and intelligent, was from a very early age far too much for his elderly *paidagôgos*, and up to every refinement of vice or mischief known to the undisciplined youth of Athens. Kleinias was worse; he was not even intelligent. Pericles tried to get rid of him once, sending him over to Ariphron's on the pretext that Alkibiades might teach him evil ways; but Ariphron in a short time satisfied himself that he could not be taught anything at all, and sent him back to Pericles. With inbreeding, the Alkmeonid brilliance was beginning to "miss a generation" here and there. The feeble Ariphron's son, Hippokrates, was good enough to be an Athenian general; but *his* sons in turn (one of whom was called Pericles) were a byword for general brutishness.

If Pericles had known what part Alkibiades was to play in Athenian history, he might have done something about it, if it were only to wring the young scapegrace's neck; but that is another story.

Meanwhile something else happened on which Xanthippos, no doubt, had hard words to say. Pericles himself, perhaps soon after the peace, had embarked on what seems to have been his only love-affair. At fifty or thereabouts, the Olympian general was captivated by the beauty, charm, and wit of a girl of about twenty,[1] a pro-

---

[1] After Pericles' death in 429 she found another protector in the general Lysikles, to whom she bore a son. Her liaison with Pericles had then lasted for a long time. It certainly began before 440, when gossip accused her of influencing Pericles against Samos, in

fessional entertainer or "companion" in the Athenian euphemism; a girl who had broken out of the drab life of an Ionian woman in the only way then possible, and made her way to the great capital: Aspasia of Miletos, who joined to striking beauty a fine and rare intelligence.

Poor Aspasia was a perfect godsend to the comic poets. Hitherto it had always been rather difficult to find any jokes about Pericles, beyond comparing his "Olympian" manner and, latterly, the powers which the Assembly heaped on him, with the powers, manner, and presumed appearance of God Almighty; or suggesting that his known partiality to wearing a helmet in public (as general) was due to a desire to conceal the way his head stuck out at the back. Now the Olympian Zeus had his Hera, who could be worked into obscene parodies of the old genealogies of the gods; or she could be thinly disguised as Omphale or Deïaneira, two of the women who softened the pride of Herakles. The average sensual Athenian was delighted to hear that Pericles had his weaknesses, and comedians and enemies were soon toying with the idea that, since he was not, after all, without tender emotions, he must be promiscuous. When young Pyrilampes brought back from a diplomatic mission to Persia a number of peacocks—never before seen in Europe—and presented some to the wives of political leaders, he was at once said to be acting as a procurer for Pericles!

It is needless to sentimentalise Aspasia. She was such as her world had made her. In the days of her prosperity she is said to have kept a household of other "girl companions," such as she herself had chosen to be, as a commercial proposition. But she made Pericles happy during the years of the making of the great buildings; she was the mother of the best of his sons; he was very much in love with her, and when he had her living with him,

---

favour of her native Miletos. Their son Pericles was approaching man's estate, according to a comedy quoted by Plutarch (almost certainly representing a scene in Hades), not long after Pericles' death. Aspasia's birth must then be placed some time in the middle sixties.

used to kiss her (people noted with avidity) on entering the house or on leaving to go to his office; and the other thing that is remembered about her was that she could hold her own in conversation with intelligent men, and that Socrates was one of those who enjoyed talking to her.

With Aspasia at his side, Pericles entered upon the final period, the great building period, of his career. His public position was unique. He was elected general fifteen years in succession, and it is likely (though *not,* as one would imagine from some modern writers, directly attested) that the actual mode of election was altered because of him. Hitherto, one general had been elected from each tribe, a survival from the days when the generals led the regiments, under the elected "War-lord." Later, all the generals were elected from the whole citizen body indiscriminately; and it is likely that a first step in this direction was taken in Pericles' time, nine generals being elected from different tribes, and *one* "from all Athenians," irrespective of what tribe might thus have two generals or what might have none. *Perhaps* also the general elected "from all Athenians" (i.e. Pericles) held in law as well as in fact a special position as General-in-Chief. In any case, the Sovereign People had now *de facto,* whether or not *de jure,* if not a recognised Prime Minister at least a Minister for Defence with an increasing voice in all matters concerning finance or foreign affairs. Among Pericles' better-known colleagues were Phormion, a daring admiral and a man of magnetic personality; Lamachos, a young swashbuckling fighting man; Hagnon, a moderate conservative politician, the only general who under the supremacy of Pericles makes an appearance with a policy of his own; and Nikias, a rich, pious owner of mining slaves, who by devotion to business and by caution in the field did his best to imitate Pericles after the great man was gone.

Another notable colleague (for long afterwards he was chosen, like Hagnon, among the "elder statesmen" to whom Athens entrusted special powers after losing almost her whole fleet in Sicily) was Sophocles. Already his chief renown was that won by his poetry; the comedian Kratinos finds it worth while to slate an archon who had dared not to select Sophocles' new plays among those for his year's dramatic festival; but like a good Athenian he attended to the daily work of the city too. In 443-442 he was a Treasurer of the League, and his name, carved by a contemporary hand, survives on the Tribute-list for that year. It is not without irony that such a man should in his business hours have been supervising the collection of tribute from an unwilling empire for the temples of Athens; should have gone from the Treasury Office to work on his famous drama of a girl's individual conscience in revolt against the total claims of the state; and directly after the triumph of his *Antigone* (spring of 441) should have been elected general, in which office it fell to him to sail with Pericles to suppress the last revolt in Pericles' lifetime by a member of the League.

A war had broken out between Samos and Miletos over the little, dependent city of Priene, an innocent victim of similar squabbles between her big neighbours since the dawn of history. Apparently the combatants did not expect Athens to intervene in this private war; nor did she, in fact, until the Milesians, getting the worst of it, complained that the Samian ruling oligarchy was disloyal. Some Samian democratic partisans gave colour to the Milesian allegations by joining their delegation. Athens, having democratised Miletos to her satisfaction ten years before, now intervened, nothing loth to do the same by powerful and too-independent Samos; for Samos was, perhaps, the strongest of all the allies; the three great islands of Samos, Chios, and Lesbos were by now the only states in the League that kept up a war-navy.

Forty ships from Athens descended upon Samos, carrying a commission which imposed a democratic constitution, took 100 hostages and dumped them on Lemnos, an island seized for Athens long since by Miltiades, and returned home, leaving a small garrison to support the Inspectors who would see the new constitution properly started. But they had under-estimated Samian pride and obstinacy. A few Samian aristocrats escaped in good time to the mainland, where they tried, successfully, to interest the Persian viceroy at Sardis, and kept up underground communications with their friends at home. Collecting some 700 mercenaries, they slipped across one night to the island, killed or arrested their opponents, and captured the Athenian garrison and commissioners. A raid on Lemnos liberated the hostages; the Athenian prisoners were handed over to the Persians; and having made all secure at home, the Samians had the assurance to embark their main forces again to take revenge on Miletos.

That they should have dared to do this is surprising; but probably they calculated that Athens, thus shocked out of a profound peace, would take time to mobilise. Sixty ships, in fact, proved to be the number which Athens could send to sea at short notice, and the Samians, who for their part could raise seventy, felt that this gave them time. They had miscalculated in their turn. Having arrived before Miletos, they were overtaken by the startling news (probably by fire signals) that an Athenian fleet was already crossing the Ægean.

Athens had taken the situation very seriously. There was no saying how far the revolt might spread in the empire; already Byzantion, though she had paid her tribute in the spring, had closed her gates against Athenians; and with the Persian viceroy Pissuthnes backing the insurgents, there was reason to fear that Persia might intervene in force. Meanwhile, however, Athenian sailors were not afraid of superior numbers. There was need for swift action. All the ten generals were ordered to sea; among the rest, Pericles, Sophocles, old Andokides, and young Glaukon, the brother-in-law of Pericles' and Andokides' sons. Pericles sailed with the first sixty ships that were ready. Even of these he had to send off detachments under his colleagues, some to scout for possible Phœnician squadrons advancing along the south coast of Asia Minor, and others to "show the flag" at Chios and Mytilene, and see that the Chian and Lesbian contingents came in on the right side. Off Tragia, the modern "Donkey Island" south of Samos, with forty-four ships, Pericles intercepted the enemy's seventy coming back from Miletos, and attacked them at once.

The odds were not so heavy as might appear, for twenty of the Samian ships were being used as transports and could not move quickly; a liability rather than an asset to the fifty that were in fighting trim. Pericles claimed a victory, in that the enemy broke off the action and fled into their harbour (the modern Tigáni, on the south coast); but he had not succeeded in cutting them off from home. All that he could do was himself to occupy a post on the island of Samos, thereby pinning down the enemy's main force.

However, his prompt action had stopped any further revolts, and presently the strain was eased. The scouts came back reporting no Phœnician fleet sighted (though five Samian ships slipped out meanwhile and sailed for Tyre to look for them); Chios and the cities of Lesbos, old enemies of Samos, sent contingents—though only twenty-five ships in all, which does not suggest enthusiasm —and forty more ships arrived from Athens. Pericles was now able to form the siege in earnest. He planted three forts round the roughly triangular city of Samos and held it under blockade.

This was not the end of the story. Presently there was another alarm of Phœnician ships approaching. Pericles took sixty ships and went to look for them; and during his absence the Samian general Melissos, a noted philosopher (he anticipated Demokritos' version of the atomic theory), surprised and defeated the remaining sixty-five ships and enjoyed a fortnight's command of the sea in which to re-provision the city. But the Phœnician ships again proved a false alarm; Pissuthnes had evidently failed to get his government to move. Sparta also—though Samian emissaries apparently got through to implore her intervention—refused to break the peace; the Corinthians, who had a small empire of their own, later took credit at Athens for asserting the principle of non-intervention in other people's imperial affairs. Pericles returned and restored the blockade. The generals for the new year, which began at midsummer, including Hagnon and Phormion, brought sixty more ships from Athens; thirty more came from Chios and Lesbos. Over 200 ships, over 40,000 men, now lay before Samos. Pericles introduced regular reliefs for the troops manning the lines, and a system of drawing for special leave, which had the attraction of a sporting event; and after a nine-months' siege and the failure of a last despairing sortie by sea, Samos surrendered on the now usual terms. Her walls were to be breached, her ships surrendered, and she was to pay by instalments the cost of the campaign; apparently, from the accounts preserved to us, the formidable total of 1,276 talents. The siege of Byzantion, which surrendered shortly after, had cost 128 talents.

During the peace that followed, Athenian seapower was not idle. Hagnon, about 437, led a powerful colony once more to Nine Ways, the scene of Leagros' disaster twenty-eight years before. All went well this time, and the coveted strategic and commercial position was held. Hagnon christened it Amphipolis, the "city surrounded"— surrounded, that is, by a wide loop of the river Strymon. Most of the colonists were non-Athenians; here, as at Thouria, Athens was organising a new, free and self-governing city for any good Greeks.

In the same decade, Pericles himself led an imposing and finely appointed naval squadron to the Black Sea coasts, Athens' vital source for supplies of corn; for neither Egypt nor the west could now be relied on. The Black Sea was also important for other commodities, such as hides, dried fish, high-grade iron from the Chalybes (in Armenia) who had magnetite ore, and low-grade slaves suitable for replacements in the silver-mines. Pericles dealt graciously with requests from the Greek colonies strewn round the shore of the great sea, offering Athens' good offices in the settlement of commercial problems and support against dangerous natives inland. Native tribes and dynasts were duly impressed by the pomp and power of the fleet and the way in which it put in where it pleased, even among the fiercest Scythians or Thracians, fearing no man. At the important colony of Sinope—an entrepôt city, where cargoes were collected for the Ægean —events played into Pericles' hands. The people were in revolt against their tyrant Timesileos, and Pericles left the young general Lamachos with thirteen ships to help them. Timesileos was duly overthrown, and subsequently, on Pericles' proposal, 600 Athenians went out to receive citizen rights at Sinope and to be settled in the houses and lands of the late tyrant's exiled supporters. Amisos (Samsun), on the coast of the Chalybes' country, also received Athenian colonists and was renamed Piræus.

Athens also strengthened her foothold on the Corinthian Gulf. The Akarnanians, in trouble with the Corinthian colonists of Ambrakia, who had seized a township called Argos on their borders, appealed to Athens for aid. Phormion was sent with thirty ships, and on his arrival tribesmen and Athenians together passed over to a vigorous offensive, captured Argos and sold the Ambrakiots as slaves. This was skating on thin ice as regards relations with Corinth; but as we have seen, Greek treaties of peace did not always cover the allies of contracting parties. The Akarnanes were delighted; Athens had no more loyal allies, and years later, after Phormion was dead, they sent to Athens to ask for "a son or kinsman of Phormion" to lead them in a later war.

Chapter 9

The Glory of Athens

THE YEARS OF PERICLES' SUPREMACY saw also the construction of the great buildings, among which the new Temple of Athene was only one, though the greatest. Released from war, Athenian energies flowed swiftly into the new channel. Plutarch gives a vivid picture of Athens under the "full employment policy":

"For Pericles wished the common people, too, to have their share in the profits of empire, but not to be paid for doing nothing; and so he brought before them the great projects for buildings, and plans that would employ many handicrafts, so that those at home, no less than those who served in the fleet and army and garrisoned the empire, might have their share in support from the public funds. For every kind of material was used—stone and bronze, ivory and gold, ebony and cypress wood—and there was work for every craft: carpenters and moulders and smiths and masons, dyers, goldsmiths, ivory-workers, embroiderers, turners; as well as the transport services, the merchants and sailors and navigators at sea, and by land the wainwrights and the breeders of oxen, the drivers, the ropemakers, the workers in flax and leather, the roadmakers and miners; and every art had, as it were, an army under its command, of the unskilled labourers, as the instrument and body of its work. Thus the need for workers disseminated prosperity through the ranks of men of every age and character. And as the buildings rose, imposing in size and matchless in their beauty and grace, while the workers vied with one another in the skill of their craftsmanship, the most surprising thing was the speed of their building; for works that one would have thought could hardly be accomplished in several successive generations were all accomplished in the prime of one man's political life."

An early item among these public works was the Middle Long Wall, already mentioned, directed by Kallikrates. Kallikrates' name also appears in a decree, about 448, where he is instructed to design a suitable door for the open-air precinct of Our Lady of Victory on the Citadel (the little Temple of Victory, that stands there now, is some twenty-five years later). It looks as though he were regularly retained by the state; and when, for the great temple of Athene of the City, we find his name joined with that of another architect, Iktinos, we may suppose that Iktinos was the artist and designer and Kallikrates the organiser and engineer.

But many other works were put in hand at the same time. In two of them Greek architects had to tackle the problem of roofing a space to accommodate a considerable audience, without use of the arch or dome; a problem which involved the difficulty of siting the necessary pillars so as not to obstruct the view. One of these was the Hall of the Mysteries at Eleusis, where the devotees witnessed those secret rites of the Corn Goddess, of which Kallias, the Torch-Bearer, was an hereditary chief priest; rites that gave hope of a glorified resurrection, like that of the "corn of wheat" that falls into the ground and dies. Iktinos was said by some later Greeks to have been the architect of this hall, "under Pericles as commissioner"; but Plutarch names three other architects (one having died during the work) and not Iktinos. The other hall was the Concert Hall, the Odeion, by an unnamed architect, with a high, tent-like, conical roof, said to have been inspired by that of Xerxes' great pavilion captured at Plataia; a building particularly near to Pericles' heart. In it were held the musical contests in lyre-playing and flute-playing and singing, which on Pericles' own proposal were at this time added to the athletic contests and procession to the Acropolis, at the four-yearly festival of Athene, the Great Panathenaia. Pericles himself was elected a Marshal of the Games at the next Panathenaia (probably 442), and personally drew up the regulations for the musical contests. Kratinos has a typical crack at him, his skull, his Odeion, his escape from *ostrakismos* and his liking for appearing in a helmet, all in three lines:

> *"And here, behold, our onion-headed Zeus*
> *Approaches, with the Odeion on his crown,*
> *Now that the ostrakon has passed him by. . . ."*

Also in the early 'forties, as we now know from the American excavations, another temple was begun on Market Hill, the little rising ground overlooking the market-place, behind the Council Chamber and the Round House where the Prytaneis on duty lived; a temple smaller and plainer than the Parthenon, yet dignified enough when seen, as it was meant to be and can now be seen again, at the top of its bank above the heart of the city. This was the temple of Hephaistos, god of the metal-workers, long known to travellers as the Theseum. Its true dedication, long suspected, has been proved by the Americans' discovery of the sites of many little forges in the area round about. Its building took longer than that of the Parthenon, and its unknown architects in the later stages borrowed some ideas from the great work of Iktinos. Perhaps one may infer that it was paid for not by state funds but chiefly by the craftsmen who lived and worked around it, in the same quarter of the old town— the Athens inhabited from that time to this—where the street of the smiths still rings witth the beating of iron and copper at the present day.

But all other buildings were outshone, then no less than now, by the great house of Athene of the City, which presently came to be called the Parthenon.

On the foundations laid long since on the highest part of the Citadel—foundations designed, as may be seen on the spot, for a rather narrower and longer building—the workmen under Kallikrates, Iktinos, and the sculptor Pheidias erected that most perfect of European buildings; there to stand intact with all its sculptures, as temple or as church of another Virgin or as mosque, until in a modern siege, in 1687, a German gunner in the service of an Italian general blew up a Turkish powder magazine inside the building, demolishing the roof and both side walls with their pillars—an episode only too typical of the history of modern Greece between the Great Powers of East and West. After that it only remained for a British Ambassador to Turkey to remove the sculptures.

There is little point in indulging in lyrical generalities about the great buildings. The way to study them is to see them under their own sky, bright in the sun or ethereal under the moon; an experience which, *experto crede,* repays any trouble. If one cannot visit Athens, a good second best is to study them in one of the many good books of photographs, some of which are, or should be, in every library. Words can only be a commentary on the experience, not a substitute; and those that follow will therefore be strictly factual.

The new temple was to be a large one, as befitted the dignity of Athens, nearly 230 feet by just over 100 (70 x 31 metres) along the top step of its foundations, and in that "Doric" style which was still the only style for Greek temples west of the Ægean; a style exceedingly simple— the translation into stone of a Bronze Age chieftain's log "hall," with porch and veranda—but enriched through generations of experience with all manner of subtleties designed to lead, rest, and delight the eye with the deliberate repetition of vertical and horizontal lines, with the contrast between restrained but elaborate ornament above and the plain colonnade below, and with the play on delicately proportioned masses of the dry Mediterranean light.

And here the refinements of the Parthenon begin.

We have spoken of vertical and horizontal lines; but, in fact, there is scarcely a horizontal or vertical line or plane, indeed not a single significant straight line, in the whole building. The fluted pillars not only taper from base to neck, giving the impression of firmness and stability; they also curve ever so little, convexly—the *entasis,* which is quite perceptible if one looks at two pillars from within, at such an angle as to leave a narrow band of light between them. But also the angle pillars are slightly thicker than the others—a fact *not* perceptible without use of the measuring tape. The later Græco-Roman architectural writers say that this was for the correction of an optical illusion in a bright light—lest the corner columns, seen against the sky, should appear *less* massive than the rest. Even more subtly, every column leans very slightly inwards, the angle columns twice as much as the others, since they are inclined in two planes. It has been calculated that—barring slight errors in execution, of which, since the builders were men, a few can be detected by measurement—the axes of all the pillars, if produced, would meet at a vertical height of about a mile. Even the level floor of the stylobate—the stepped foundation on which the pillars stand—is not really level at all. It rises ever so slightly in a gentle bulge—not a true curve—towards the centre of each side; two-and-three-quarter inches in the middle of each end, and, even more gently, about four inches in each long side. For the sake of drainage, some may prosaically suspect; but this still leaves the execution of these refinements by the masons and stone-cutters a marvel much greater than the conception of the idea; and in favour of the view that it was meant to have æsthetic significance is the fact that the whole entablature—all that rests upon the pillars—rises towards the centre of each side, parallel to the lift of the stylobate.

These refinements, invisible or all but invisible to the casual eye, do in fact go far to account for the unique satisfactoriness of the simple lines of the Parthenon. That they were deliberately designed to that end is the tradition reported by the Roman Vitruvius, who drew on Greek architecural writers. They were not invented by Iktinos out of nothing; entasis of the pillars is normal in Doric building; curvature of the stylobate is found in the sturdy archaic temple at Corinth, built a hundred years before. But they were not invariably found; in the Hephaistos temple, for example, the floor is flat; and their success is best seen simply by looking at the two temples, one after the other. The Parthenon is to the Hephaisteion as the music of Bach to ordinary, good music of his day. The difference is the measure of what we owe to the individual man Iktinos, the artist who was backed by Pericles.

By 438 the Parthenon was complete, with most of its sculpture. So swiftly was Greek art developing that, even within those ten years' work, the combats of Greeks and Centaurs, Gods and Giants, and the like (civilisation *versus* barbarism), which filled the square *metopes* above the colonnade outside, are perceptibly less mature in style than the frieze, high up on the wall of the "cell" or temple, inside the colonnade.

The whole of this work, says Plutarch, was organised and directed by Pheidias, the sculptor friend of Pericles. Pheidias also wrought the huge, severe, bronze statue of the armed Athene that stood near the entrance to the rock; a figure sixty feet high, the gleam of whose spear and helmet were visible to sailors on a clear day many miles out at sea. Pericles himself—we learn from a piece of current gossip—was a frequent visitor to the workshops. For an artist to be not only patronized but on personal terms of friendship with a great statesman was something new in Greek society. It is noteworthy that while almost all the great poets of Greece in the sixth and fifth centuries move in the high society of their cities, the artists are generally socially obscure. They were artisans; respected for their skill, but "below the salt" in our old feudal expression. The whole position is typical of the contrast between the aristocratic Greek attitude to the work of the mind of man and the work of his hands. Under Pheidias must have worked many of these nameless artisan-sculptors—the same men who carved the tombstones that are treasured in modern museums. Pheidias' work on the Parthenon is an example of the fact that in art also, as in other human achievements, the genius depends for his opportunities on the whole condition, the whole level of achievement, of society in his time.

But from Pheidias' association with the Periclean circle sprang, we may well believe, one thing unique in Greek sculpture: the choice of a subject for the frieze of the Parthenon.

Greek "public" art—architectural sculpture—like Greek

poetry except for personal lyric and elegy, chose its subjects from the traditional mythology. This is not to say
that Greek poetry and art were academic or out of
touch with life; far from it. The myths expressed and
typified the ordinary people's hopes, fears, and aspira-
tions, conscious or subconscious, and had grown up and
gained popularity for that reason. But for this very reason,
that the myths of the gods and heroes adequately expressed man's deepest feelings, it was rare for scenes of
ordinary, contemporary life to penetrate into major Greek
poetry or art. Satisfaction with the mythology as an expression of man's feelings was normal. What was rare
was the feeling that "modern" contemporary life could be
a suitable subject for great poetry or art.

Such a feeling implies the realisation that events of
contemporary life can have the same universal significance as the deeds of mythic heroes; a realisation achieved
in Greece by a few rare spirits, or by a whole population
on rare occasions. The divine smith in Homer inlays the
hero's shield with scenes of daily life; but other compara-
ble descriptions of works of art are always confined to scenes
from mythology. Hesiod had the vision of the poetry—
that is, the significance—of daily life, and held it long
enough to make it a poem of the Farmer's Year; but the
school of poets that followed him applied even didactic—
"instructive"—poetry exclusively to teaching the mythology. In Athenian tragedy, Phrynichos at least twice,
Æschylus at least once, had had a poet's vision of the
vital signficance of the Persian Wars; but it had faded in
the light of common day, among the more complex, less
single-hearted moods of the years that followed. Greek
painting—almost wholly lost to us—also sometimes rendered "modern" subjects; there was a painting of the
Battle of Marathon by the great artist Polygnotos in the
Painted Colonnade in the Agorá; but sculpture hardly
ever. Pheidias' achievement—or that of Periclean, Pheid-
ian Athens—is the best example of all the raising of contemporary life, in the artist's vision, to the "godlike"
plane. Round the Parthenon outside the colonnade, indeed, one saw the usual combats of heroes and centaurs,

Greeks and Trojans, Greeks and Amazons, Gods defeating Giants; the mythic symbols of Hellenism triumphing through struggle. But if one looked up at the frieze inside the pillars, one saw that Athens, greatly daring, had chosen for the subject of this band of sculpture—Athenians at worship. One would like to know whether the Assembly debated that choice.

The subject is, in fact, the Panathenaic Procession, the annual procession (conducted with especial splendour every fourth year), of Athenians to visit the city's goddess; the occasion for which was, by a charming archaic tradition, the presentation to the goddess of her annual new frock. (It is a reflection still a little shocking to some old-fashioned classicists, that ancient Greeks painted their statues, and even sometimes hung real clothes on them.) The robe has been woven and embroidered by girls of old Athenian families; and here is the procession. Over the west door it is in preparation; along the side-walls it is in full career. At the east end the grave, bearded priests and magistrates have already arrived, and stand leaning each on his staff, awaiting the rest of the company. Next come maidens, no less grave, carrying in pitchers and baskets the wine and oil, the wheaten cakes, meal for the meal offering, and other requisites for the sacrifice. After them come the victims, the rams and cattle, who will die as the central act of the day's proceedings (one likes to forget that an essential part of a Greek festival was the creation of a reeking shambles at the altar before the temple); then more citizens: musicians; men carrying green sprays of Athene's tree, the olive; chariots—an old-fashioned engine of war, still keeping its place, as so often, in ceremonial; and lastly the young "knights" on their sturdy, thick-necked Thessalian horses, reining in their mettlesome, curvetting mounts to the slow foot-pace of the procession.

Such was the cortège that every year passed up the steep zig-zag road, up the west end of the Rock; with other elements too—the Robe itself, set as a sail (characteristically of the naval state) on a model ship, which was mounted on a wagon and hauled laboriously up the well-worn zig-zags; and the Foreign Residents, to whom Athens, as they could no longer become citizens and were still wanted by Athenian economy, gave an honourable place in the scheme of things. They were distinguished in the procession by a "uniform" of red cloaks. Over the east door, finally, where the head of the procession has arrived, sit the Gods: Father Zeus, Queen Hera, Athene, Artemis, Apollo, Aphrodite and her son Eros, the "delicate" boy-god under his mother's parasol; just as many in the procession pictured them actually sitting in some far-off Olympian home, looking down on their worshippers.

The world has no festival now to match the Panathenaia, with its procession and singing, its concerts in the new Hall and sports outside the walls, with competitions between the greatest musicians and athletes of the day; stateliest of all the great or little *panegyreis* or "gatherings" that took place some day in the year at every Greek shrine or city, famous or obscure. But one may still savour the spirit if not the form of it at a Greek festival, and realise the Greek capacity for utter absorption in a rite that is at once a duty and a joy; best of all perhaps at Athens at Easter under the Paschal moon, when at midnight all light their tapers, one from another, because Christ is risen, and go out to tell the news—so that rivers of fire pour down from Lykabettos and along every street.

The Great Panathenaia of 438 witnessed the dedication of the Athene Parthenos (Athene the Virgin), the great gold-and-ivory statue—gold for the robes and armour, ivory for the face and hands—wrought by Pheidias for the temple. We know little of it to-day. It is long since that ivory was broken and that gold flowed molten into some barbarian mint. The type of the surviving copies is well called by Beazley "that vulgar little souvenir." But one remembers the saying of the Roman critic Quintilian, about the great Zeus which Pheidias made later at Olympia, that "it seemed to add something to the received religion."

A more prosaic ancient traveller says that the Zeus was so huge that, though the temple at Olympia is very large, it seemed out of proportion. We have no such stricture on the Parthenos; yet that also was gigantic—nearly forty feet high, including its base. Such colossi scarcely fit into some over-scholastic schemes of ideas about Greek "moderation." The reason is, of course, that such ideas are over-simplified. Modesty was for men, not for gods, or for work done in their honour. The Parthenon itself is a building large enough to deceive a casual eye as to its distance, when seen without its immediate surroundings across rolling country from the south-east; when new, in flashing white marble with details picked out in paint, it must have been overwhelming—especially to eyes of its day, not inured to Gothic cathedrals or New York skyscrapers. And so also with the Athene Parthenos. Passing from the glare of white marble in the sun outside into the dark temple, lit only through the door,[1] one found oneself, as one's eyes grew accustomed to the dimness, before that colossal Presence; the gold and ivory glimmering softly in the half-light.

Pheidias was justifiably proud of his *chef-d'œuvre;* so much so that he hit on a novel plan for "signing" his work, as medieval artists often did, by introducing unobtrusive portraits of himself and his patron Pericles, among the fighting warriors on Athene's shield: Pheidias as a bald old man, hurling a rock with both hands; Pericles handsome, and quite recognisable if one was in the secret, though his upraised arm came in front of his face. Could anyone object?

Yes; partly from the old feeling that it was impious to mix the mundane with the divine, and partly from sheer, crude jealousy of Pericles and Pheidias, some people did. The building of the Parthenon did not pass without what one must regretfully call a normal amount of quarrelling and slander, and Pheidias got from the support of Pericles, not only magnificent opportunities and reflected glory, but reflected envy. There must have been scores of fellow-workers who fancied that, given the chance, they could have done quite as well as Pheidias, and who per-

---

[1] Some have suggested a diffused light penetrating through the marble slats of the roof; but those that have been found are one-and-a-half inches thick.

haps could have done nearly as well; and as for Pericles, his unrivalled position inevitably aroused jealousy, among a nation in which, as the Greeks say nowadays, "everyone is a captain." Someone with a genius for slander accounted for Pericles' and other people's frequent visits to the workshops, and for Pericles' friendship with Pheidias, with the theory that Pheidias made himself useful to Pericles by arranging assignations in the tool-shed with various lady visitors; and soon after the dedication of the Parthenos, a storm burst.

First Pheidias was accused of stealing gold entrusted to him for the statue. That, at least, was soon refuted. The gold plates were detachable, and they were simply taken down and weighed. (Parts of the accounts for the statue, which first and last cost over 700 talents—4,200,000 drachmas—are still extant.) But then someone, examining the details of the great shield, identified Pheidias' two little portraits of Pericles and himself. The cry of impiety —"sacrilege"—was raised; a matter on which the superstitious Assembly was always sensitive. Pheidias is said to have been imprisoned; if so, Pericles got him out, like Anaxagoras before him, and he left Athens, never to return. Plutarch, indeed, says that he died in prison; but it seems certain that he survived, after the dedication of the Parthenos in 438, to work in the Peloponnese on his great Zeus at Olympia. The prison in which Pheidias died may, indeed, have been simply a war-time place of internment; for we know that the Athenians, and may infer that others, did arrest enemy nationals when war broke out again in 431.

It was a tragic end to the work for Athens of Athens' greatest sculptor; but the adornment of the Acropolis was not checked. A brilliant new architect, Mnesikles, was now commissioned to provide the Citadel with a worthy entrance-portal; and in 437 work on this building, the Propylaia, was already under way. It was an ambitious project. The zig-zag carriage-way passed, on the brow of the Rock, through a Doric colonnade, and under a marble, coffered ceiling supported on Ionic columns; a cunning mixture of the two styles, since the Ionic pillars, traditionally taller and more slender than Doric, could reach the ceiling without being made disproportionate to the sturdy Doric columns that only had to reach and support a lintel. This entrance, the portal proper, was to be flanked, it appears, by two symmetrical wings. A square hall on each side of the entrance would give the effect, from without, of a solid and massive buttress supporting the colonnade at either end; while internally, the halls would be used as picture galleries. Finally, each wing would be covered by a further colonnade on the side facing the summit. The building is said to have cost over 2,000 talents, the price of twelve million skilled-labourer-days; and that though, for reasons which will appear, it was never finished as Mnesikles had intended.

Before the Propylaia were finished, indeed, the shadows were falling upon Pericles and all that he stood for; and yet even so, the Acropolis as he left it, with the addition of two smaller but exquisite temples built by men who remembered him, remains one of the great wonders of the world. Plutarch, after remarking that, as a rule, rapid construction is not conducive to the highest beauty, thus sums up:

"And this is the more cause to marvel at the buildings of Pericles, that were made in so little time to last for so long. For their beauty they seemed venerable as soon as they were built, and in freshness to this day they seem as though newly finished; such a bloom of newness is there upon them, keeping them, to the eye, untouched by time, as though those works had in them an evergreen spirit and a soul of unfading youth."

Chapter 10

Spirit of a Democracy

BELOW THE ACROPOLIS the everyday life of Athens seethed and chattered, down in the crowded streets round the Agorá—the "Place of Gathering," much more than merely a "market-place"—where people from every part of the Greek world swelled the crowds of Athenians, slaves, and resident foreigners, and deputations from the Empire waited wearily for the Sovereign People to find time to deal with their business.

As an anti-democratic pamphlet explains, the hard-worked Council of Five Hundred was suffering from acute congestion of business. To begin with, the author remarks drily, the Athenians have got more holy-days to work through than any other state in Greece, and on all of these both government offices and law courts are shut. (One has to remember that Greece had no Sundays.) Then the Council had business connected with defence, finance (including the assessment and receipt of tribute), legislation, internal affairs, imperial affairs, pensions to war-orphans, and prison administration. It had to see (literally) to the satisfactory condition of the temples and of the naval dockyards. It had also a good deal of judicial work to review and, if necessary, send to a jury; magistrates' accounts, the examination of candidates for office before they were admitted to the draw, cognizance of unusual crimes (probably deciding which court should try them), and the hearing of appeals against their assessment by any of the several hundred rich men who in any year, as a regular part of the taxation system, were charged with a year's maintenance of a warship or the provision of a chorus for one of the festivals. It is quite true, admits our Athenian, as though in answer to a question, that while some foreigners are kept waiting for months, others by paying "bakshish" get their business done early; but no amount of "bakshish," he adds, would alter the fact that both Council and Courts have too much to do. Meanwhile Athens finds it highly profitable to have so many foreigners in town, not only publicly (e.g. it increases the landing-tolls at Piræus), but privately; it is "good for trade," especially for people with lodgings to let, or transport or slaves for hire.

It is a lively affair, this little anonymous pamphlet. It has come down to us among the essays of Xenophon, who was not born until about the time that Pericles died. But several points in it make it quite clear that it was written within a few years of Pericles' death and while the Athenian democracy and empire still stood as he left them. Possibly it might be by another Xenophon, a cavalry-commander of Pericles' time, who was a general, and was killed in action, in 429. Its title is *The Athenian Commonwealth*. Its interest lies in the fact that it gives a contemporary, Athenian, *hostile* view of the democracy, and that in spite of himself the author—an Athenian still, though no democrat—cannot withhold grudging admiration of the efficiency with which Demos looks after his class-interests. It gives us the best possible answer to the question whether Athens, in whose government aristocrats played so large a part, can really have been a democracy in practice. If we had only, say, Pericles' own view of the matter, we might suppose that he was idealising. The evidence of this author, whom Gilbert Murray pleasantly christened the Old Oligarch, that the Athenians were altogether too democratic (and, incidentally, too soft to their slaves) is the best possible evidence both for their democracy and for their kindliness.

The essay is clearly meant for a foreign audience; perhaps originally an impromptu lecture to an aristocratic political club, with additions in reply to questions. This would account for its being careless in style and loosely put together. Its tone is one of hard-boiled but light-hearted political realism, not yet soured by the strains and stresses of war; and its main thesis is that Demos knows very well what it is doing in all those democratic proceedings that looked so queer to the governing classes of

Sparta or Thebes. Consequently there is not a hope of overthrowing the democracy from within.

"I do not approve of the Athenian Constitution," he begins, "because by choosing it they have chosen to give the rabble a better time than the decent folk; but since they have chosen it, I propose to show that they take sound measures to preserve their constitution, even in matters where the rest of Greece thinks they are going wrong. First of all, it is perfectly fair that the poor and the commons have advantages over the nobles and the rich, for this reason, that it is the people who row the ships and give the city its power . . . much more than armoured troops and the nobles and the decent classes. For this reason they think it is right that all should have an equal chance of office, by election or by lot, and that any citizen who wishes should have the right to speak" [in the Assembly]. "They do not choose the generals and cavalry-colonels by lot; for the people know that it is better for them that they should not hold these positions, but let those hold them who are best able; . . . but they do seek to hold those offices which are concerned with pay and personal economic advantage."

So, too, in the Council and Assembly: "If they let only the better citizens" [or upper classes] "speak, or sit in the Council, these people would devise measures in the interest of those like them, and not of the people; but as it is, any low type who wishes gets up and devises what is best for himself and his like. . . . They know very well that such a man's untutored cunning and loyalty will produce better results than the decent citizen's virtue and wisdom and disloyalty. A city so run may not be ideally the best, but that is how to preserve a democracy; for what the people want is not the best possible order, with themselves in slavery, but freedom and control of the government. Disorder is a minor consideration."

For the same reason, he goes on (reverting to the point three times in some fifteen pages), the Athenian democracy backs up the proletariat in all the cities of the Empire; "for if the rich and the better classes prevail in the Cities, the rule of the people will not last long at Athens."

When Athens supported the "best people" in Boiotia or at Miletos, he adds, or helped Sparta against the Messenians, the results were disastrous. One may remark that all these mistakes belong to the years before 450. Athens had learnt her lesson.

There is a good deal of charm about the candour with which the Old Oligarch blows the gaff about political realities. It is apparent that he would not have found much to surprise him about the politics of modern Europe.

Among details which he explains, in passing, is the state organisation of festivals and other amenities. Pericles, as we have seen, took a deep personal interest in this movement, which shared all that Greece had to offer of art and music with the average man. The Old Oligarch shows us that it extended to other amenities too: "The people, seeing that poor men cannot individually afford sacrifices and feasts and to build temples and have a fine and glorious city to live in, have devised the means to possess these amenities. The city, publicly, sacrifices many victims, and it is the people who divide up the meat and feast upon it. And athletic-grounds with baths and dressing-rooms are things which *some* rich men possess privately; but now the people builds for itself wrestling-schools and dressing-rooms and bath-houses, and the masses make more use of these than the well-to-do few." It appears that in this respect, if not in others, the Athenian democracy might be called socialist.

Elsewhere the writer refers without details to some legislation against private musical and athletic clubs (probably from fear that they might be used as cover for activities against the democracy), and to the well-known system of financing the great choral and athletic festivals by "soaking the rich." He also explains the connection between democracy and the unparalleled freedom of satire allowed to comedy. "They do not allow writers to satirise the people, that they may not hear gibes at themselves." (And yet Aristophanes is constantly mocking at Demos, and once at least put an Athenian John Bull on the stage.) "But of individuals, they let anyone satirise anyone, knowing quite well that the victims will not be, as a rule, men of the people, but somebody rich or aristocratic or powerful. It is rare for poor men or democrats to be attacked, and when they are it is generally for pushing themselves forward and trying to set themselves up above the people, so that no one is sorry when people like that are laughed at." (It appears from an old commentator on Aristophanes that Athens did once—during the crisis of the Samian War—legislate to restrict the freedom of comedy; but the restrictions, whatever they were, were relaxed after a couple of years.)

But to us the most striking detail in the pamphlet is certainly that about the treatment of slaves: "Slaves and aliens are extremely undisciplined at Athens. You are not allowed to hit them, and a slave will not get out of your way. The reason is that if the law did allow a slave to be struck by a free man . . . it would often happen that one struck an Athenian by mistake; for they are no better dressed and no better to look at." Lest we should idealise Athens unduly, it must be added that one must not forget the unhappy low-grade slaves who worked probably ten-hour shifts, as shown by the duration of their oil-lamps, in the stifling shafts of the silver-mines; and that if a slave was required to give evidence for a court of law, that evidence was given under torture. His master's permission, however, had to be given before the slave could be thus questioned; and it was frequently refused. It is clear from inscriptions, too, that many Athenians worked alongside their slaves, fluting pillars for the great temples, for example, or otherwise at the same work; and, at least in an emergency, slaves, citizens and hired men from the Empire would row together in the fleet.

Altogether the Old Oligarch's picture agrees very well with the charming satire on democracy in Plato's *Republic*. There, too, we have the indignant testimony that slaves are "no less free than those who bought them." And, Plato adds, "the extent to which domestic animals are freer there than in other states has to be seen to be believed. The bitch is as good as her mistress, as the proverb puts it, and the horses and donkeys, accustomed to march with all the dignity of freedom, bump into the man who meets them in the street if he doesn't get out of the way." (Anyone who has met a string of Greek donkeys on a mountain path or in a crowd will appreciate Plato's sentiments.) There is the same anarchy as between old and young: "The father tries to be like his child, and is afraid of his sons, and the son like his father, and there is no respect or reverence for age—for the sake of freedom; . . . and the old play down to the young and . . . imitate them, so as not to be thought strict and unsporting." Plato, it is true, belongs to the next generation, and to a "post-war" age at that; but all that we hear of the youth of Alkibiades, who was brought up in Pericles' household, suggests that the modern spirit which Plato notices among bright young people was well developed already.

Women too, jeers Plato, are on an equality with men. It is rather surprising that he should object to this, since it is a feature of his own ideal Republic. Moreover it was *not* a feature of life at Athens, where women were married off at adolescence to husbands of thirty, and had next to no education and no political rights. But it was, one may notice, in Athens—not least, in Plato himself —that Greeks began to discuss the question of equality between the sexes; and the fact that Aristophanes devotes three of his twelve extant plays to "Women in Parliament" or cognate subjects, shows that feminism was a live issue, a theme at least for jokes, within his lifetime.

"The whole place is full to bursting with liberty," Plato sums up, ". . . and people get so touchy that if the slightest restraint is applied they make an outcry and consider it unendurable; in the end, as you know, they will not even obey the laws." He has already commented that if you want to hold any position in a democracy and there is a law that disqualifies you, that is nothing to stop you. No doubt he is thinking of the labourer class at Athens, who, if they stood for the archonship, were merely written down as small-holders.

Yet even Plato, for all his irony, feels, like the Old Oligarch, a certain affection for the democracy of his youth. He makes the democratic state much more attractive than any of the other "faulty" cities, which he describes as a foil to his ideal Republic; though in his scheme of things democracy is a worse form of constitution than capitalist plutocracy, which in turn is worse than feudal aristocracy; and his typical democratic man, who flits with engaging versatility from enjoyment to austerity or from philosophy to soldiering, is simply the democratic Athenian drawn from life.

Athens too was not only a focus radiating the city's own contributions to civilisation. She was also continually receiving and welcoming influences from abroad. The years of Pericles' supremacy were the early years of the Age of the Sophists.

Sophos being the Greek word for wise or, in the old sense of the English word, cunning, the verb *sophizo* meant to profess wisdom, or to make or, as the Americans say, put you wise. A *Sophistes* had meant in earlier times an exponent of any form of "cunning" or specialised knowledge. It was now coming increasingly to mean an exponent of higher education; in short, a professor.

The continued dissemination of philosophic and scientific ideas had created a demand from a considerable public, chiefly young men of the leisured classes, for information as to what it was all about. Simultaneously in Sicily, where a democracy on the Kleisthenic model was established at Syracuse about 470, men had started to study methodically the art of speaking, increasingly important in the new democratic law courts and assemblies: how to turn a sentence rhythmically and pleasantly, and above all how to make the most of the strong points in a case and gloss over the weak ones. Since the new scientific ideas were lethal to a literal belief in the Olympic gods and the old mythology; since the ethics deduced by some people from the new philosophy amounted to maintaining that the law of the jungle was "natural" and the laws of the state only "conventional"; since the purveyors of the new knowledge found their best-paying pupils among young aristocrats, interested in holding their own amid—or against—the rising tide of democracy, and since their livelihood depended on popularity and quick results, the Sophists soon acquired a rather sinister reputation. This was unjust to several of the best and most famous of them, such as Gorgias, of Leontinoi in Sicily, who came to Athens in 427 in connection with the renewal of the old alliance, or Protagoras, from Abdera on the Thracian coast; but it was true that both these intelligent and honourable men had deduced, from the diverse results so far attained by philosophers, philosophic views of their own which amounted to a far-reaching scepticism. As regards ethics, it is from the alleged teaching of the sophists that a young rip in Aristophanes derives the view that it is what the animals do, and therefore "natural," and therefore right and proper, that he should beat up his old father as soon as he is strong enough. Alkibiades, Pericles' ward, brilliant and unscrupulous, is the typical product of Athens in the new age.

Athenian citizens had other things to do than to become sophists; but the age of reason was affecting Athenian public life none the less. A new dramatist had made his début in 455, and was now second only to Sophocles in popular favour. Like the early Shaw, he at once enthralled and infuriated his audiences by his use of the new ideas; by his psychology, especially of women, which some people thought morbid; by his realism—his use of rags and dirt, for example, in dressing characters reduced to slavery or other adversity (this shocked people very much like realism in a modern production of a play on a "sacred" subject), and by his use of the "sophistic" tricks in the set debates between his characters, which he was fond of staging. This was Euripides. There was a grave, thoughtful man beginning to be known in politics—a relation of the exiled Thoukydides, but a supporter of Pericles—who prided himself on his power to see things objectively, and when people got into a panic about an eclipse of the sun or moon as a portent of divine displeasure, remarked drily that it was curious that these things only happened about the turn of the month or at the full moon respectively. He was Thucydides the historian. There was an ugly, snub-nosed, strongly built man of working-class origin, who combined a devastating power of destructive criticism with a conviction that there must be a basis for morality somewhere. He was beginning to be popular with the bright young people, who learned his tricks and took them home to try out on father. This was Socrates. All these three were products of the Kleisthenic democracy; for Euripides as well as Socrates was of lowly origin, and Thucydides would have been excluded by the citizenship law of 451 had it been passed earlier. He was of noble descent but one of his great-grandmothers—the mother of Kimon—was Thracian.

The chief exponent of the new oratory in Athens was Antiphon, the first Athenian whose speeches were written down and treasured by students as examples of how to do it. He was a conservative, even a reactionary; a member of the "country party" which championed the rights of the "allies" against the radical imperialists. He became a great "counsel for the allies." A speech survives, which he wrote for delivery by a young man of Mytilene, accused of the murder of an Athenian. We hear the names of others, "on the Tribute of Samothrace," "on the Tribute of Lindos" (in Rhodes), presumably appealing against the assessments of those cities, and prosecuting Laispodias, a general and politician who was a distant connection of Pericles. From them, Byzantine lexicographers quote place-names and technical terms: "Collectors . . . taxation-group . . . separate assessment . . . Amphipolis . . . inspectors." One seems to be overhearing snatches of the proceedings in those busy law courts round the Agorá.

Antiphon also wrote "fair-copies," or school debating speeches for mock homicide trials, for the edification of his pupils. One set of four (two speeches for each side) deals with a case of accidental killing—a javelin-throwing accident on a sports-ground—and is interesting as showing how the age of reason was trying to deal with the pre-rational customs left over from a still recent past. There is no suggestion of malice or of anything but pure accident in Antiphon's imaginary case; but blood has been shed; the boy who threw the javelin is *aitios*—"responsible" or "guilty"—of the death of one of the people; and so the next of kin, the father of the boy who has been killed, without rancour, but to satisfy the ghost, or public opinion, or his own conscience, according to one's way of looking at it, demands that he shall go into exile. The father of the defendant, in reply, does not waste his breath in complaining that these old customs are irrational; Antiphon knows that there is no escape that way. He simply argues that his son is not *aitios* at all, because when he had already thrown his javelin, within the limits of the proper range, the little boy who was killed ran, playing, into the way. He is therefore *aitios of his own death*.

This question of fatal accidents at sport particularly exercised the minds of thoughtful Greeks, because it brought up clearly and sharply the whole question of blood-pollution. Œdipus in Sophocles' play had killed his father in a fight on a highway, unknowing; but that makes no difference to his sense of having incurred an appalling pollution. It must have added yet more to the pity and terror of that drama when first performed, that its audience were just beginning to feel—the poet and his friends of Pericles' circle, especially—that the old doctrine could be hideously unjust to innocent people. We hear of another famous debate on a javelin accident in which the participants were the famous sophist, Protagoras, and Pericles himself.

Protagoras visited Athens some time in the late thirties. Plato, who was then not yet born, has given a vivid imaginative picture of the brilliant house-party of sophists at the house of the young Kallias, grandson of the old ambassador; but it is "historical fiction," not history. Kallias did not succeed to the family property till after his half-brothers, the sons of Pericles, who appear "among those present," were dead. Plato seldom if ever troubled about exact dates in these "dramatic settings" of his dialogues. Here he combines the famous house-party (which is historical, but took place about 422 and was parodied in a comedy at that time) with Protagoras' earlier visit in

Pericles' lifetime; and his speakers discuss another play which, as Plato could have found out from the official records, was not produced till 421.

Pericles might "never have time" to go to parties, but he had time to receive Protagoras. No doubt, since Anaxagoras had left Athens, he missed the long philosophical talks with his old friend. The subject of a recent javelin-accident arose; and for the better part of a day the theorist and the veteran statesman discussed the enthralling question, Who was *aitios?* We are not told that any final conclusion was reached; but three views were exhaustively canvassed, and between them they represent all the theories current in Greece at the time. They were: (1) that the javelin-thrower was *aitios;* (2) that it was the javelin itself; and (3) that it was the men who organised the games. The first was the "common-sense" view, which bore so hardly upon the accidental homicide. The second, the imputation of responsibility to an inanimate object, was a curiosity of jurisprudence to which Athenian law could actually resort to shift the "guilt" off the shoulders of innocent people—for instance, when at a certain festival it was necessary to sacrifice the old friend of man, a ploughing ox. The third solution, worthy of the two brilliant men who threshed it out together, was probably the solution at which a modern jury would have arrived: that responsibility attached to the organisers of the games, for their neglect to make more careful regulations.

Sometimes "sophistic" arguments in which Pericles found himself involved were not quite so congenial.

"Could you tell me exactly how you would define Law?" Alkibiades asked him one day. "Certainly," said Pericles, glad to have his skittish young ward asking such a suitable question. "Because I do want to know," went on the boy, his beautiful face aglow with innocence; "because one keeps hearing people being praised for being law-abiding, and one can't deserve that praise when one isn't sure what Law is, can one?"

Alkibiades had evidently been talking to Socrates, who was always keen on definitions.

"Well," said Pericles, "that's not a very difficult question. Everything is Law that has been voted by the People in Parliament Assembled, prescribing or forbidding any class of actions."

"But supposing it is not the whole people that votes, but a minority, as in an oligarchy, is that still Law?"

"Yes; everything is called Law that is enacted by an established Government."

"But if a despot makes enactments for the citizens of a state, is that called Law?"

This was getting a bit awkward. However, Pericles answered: "Yes, if he is the government."

"But, Pericles," asked Alkibiades, "in that case, what is lawlessness and the rule of force? Isn't that found when the stronger imposes his will on the weaker, by power and not by persuasion?"

"Yes."

"Well, then surely the enactments of a despot, who rules without the consent of the governed, are the negation of Law?"

"Yes, they are," said Pericles. "I withdraw what I said before about a despot's commands being Law."

"Then what about an oligarchy's commands, if it legislates for the people without their consent?"

Pericles said: "Everything which one forces another to do, without gaining his consent by persuasion, seems to me to be arbitrary force rather than lawful."

"Well, then," said Alkibiades, looking more innocent than ever, "when the people, being stronger than the rich, legislate for the rich without *their* consent, is that arbitrary?"

"Ah, Alkibiades," said the general, "I was clever at that sort of subtlety when I was your age!"

"I wish I had known you when you were at your best," said Alkibiades.

Even the story of Pericles' talk with Protagoras was, in fact, first given to the world on a painful occasion. Young Xanthippos, exasperated by his wife's nagging and unable, on his allowance, to give her "the standard of life to which she was accustomed," at last borrowed money, using his father's name. In due course the creditor asked Pericles for his money back, and the story came out; whereat Pericles, probably foreseeing a lawsuit anyhow and preferring to take the offensive, not only refused to pay, but prosecuted the creditor for trying to obtain money by false pretences. Xanthippos found himself compelled to give evidence on behalf of his money-lending friend, and the Protagoras story is part of the evidence he gave, in the course of an effort to show that his father was hopelessly eccentric (a matter on which most of Athens was already convinced, but always delighted to hear more evidence). But Xanthippos also said something far worse, namely that his father had been making love to his own, Xanthippos', wife; a story at once poohpoohed by most decent people, but carefully picked up by Stesimbrotos of Thasos, and put into his *Memoirs*. It is, no doubt, from the same source that we have the allegation that Pericles squandered his substance on Aspasia. Xanthippos had never felt any affection for his father, and he remained very bitter against him throughout the few more years that they were both to live.

Pericles certainly had his share of personal troubles; but he usually managed to rise superior to them, into that Olympian calm of contemplation which so much annoyed those unable to share it. From some time during his "reign" comes the story of how once he was pursued with shouting and abuse all day by some man with a real or fancied grievance; how he took no notice of him throughout business hours, and how finally at sunset the man—presumably a lunatic—followed him home. At his door, the Olympian turned and had his revenge, saying to one of his servants: "Take a lamp, and see this gentleman home."

Chapter 11

A Shadow in the West

PERICLES' POSITION might be unique, but he never ceased
to be attacked. The prosecutions of his friends were not
only spite; they were, as we have seen, political moves
intended to weaken Pericles' position by "revelations."
Damon, Anaxagoras, Pheidias—they had all gone; and
then came the unkindest cut of all, an attack on Aspasia.
The prosecutor was the comic poet Hermippos, always
one of her fiercest assailants; the charge, "impiety"—
possibly she had been giving her girls the names of the
Muses—but Hermippos threw in for good measure the
charge of assisting Pericles in amours with free-born
women. Since she was doubly disqualified from speaking
in her own defence—as an alien and as a woman—Pericles appeared for her. The violence and the foulness of
the attacks made on the woman he loved, out of jealousy
of his work, broke through even his armour of restraint,
and when he spoke, he wept. The jury, experiencing an
agreeable "revulsion of feeling," acquitted Aspasia.

Pericles had won, as usual; but there was something
new and dangerous about the attacks of the 'thirties. Hermippos a little later joins in attacking Pericles with a
politician who was anathema to the tory Aristophanes:
one Kleon, owner of a tanning business, who was by way
of representing the views of the people; not exactly of the
poor—the official records show a man, probably his
father, paying for a victorious choir at a festival in 469—
but of the Plain Man. Kleon, violent, able, a good finan-
cier, with a deep mistrust of intellectuals, was a portent;
Pericles, who had hitherto always followed that well-
known maxim for radicals, never to let his left flank be
turned, was being attacked from the left at last.

This is what distinguishes Pericles' last political battles
from those earlier frays with Thoukydides or Kimon.

We must remind ourselves again of the political alignments in Athens. The "conservative party" in the Assembly was a country party, supported by landed proprietors, whether rich squires or simply peasants; pacific, because in war it might see its farms spoiled by a Peloponnesian army; unenthusiastic about foreign trade, which merely lowered the price of farm produce; its extreme members anti-democratic, and its leaders disposed to stand up for the rights of allies, largely from sympathy with the rich men in "the Cities," who paid the League tribute. Against this party stood the democratic imperialists, a town ("bourgeois") party, consisting of all who made a living out of foreign trade or imperial service (including service on juries) and were aware that their lives depended upon imported food. Pericles had risen with the rise of the latter party; but he knew that its most dangerous fault was over-confidence, readiness to embark on distant adventures that were often terribly costly in blood and treasure. So far as was consistent with keeping the Empire (as in the war with Samos) and securing the people's food supply (as in the Black Sea expedition), Pericles was for peace; he had worked consistently to that end, at least since the days of the Egyptian disaster. Nearest to his heart was an ideal Athens, yet an Athens not far from realisation in the singing and the athletics, the lyrical dramas and processions, of the great festivals; the Athens, one may fairly say, of the Parthenon frieze; Athens as—in his own phrase—"an education to Greece." Surely in the end, without more fighting, every Greek community must see how much the greatest and fairest city of the world was Athens, and join willingly in one great League, of which Athens would be the head?

Pericles over-estimated the strength of his own ideals as a political motive. He may also have overlooked the fact that the prosperous commercial life of Athens must tend to expand. Where there are four prosperous shoemakers, it is only natural if a fifth opens a business, and then if the original four look out for more customers. Athens controlled, directly and politically, the channels of Greek trade through the Ægean, with the Black Sea and the Levant; but she had also (we can tell from the distribution of Attic pottery) long since penetrated the markets of Italy and Sicily, even to distant Etruria and Carthage. Where trade had gone, many dreamed of planting the flag; and in their eyes the colony at Thouria, the alliances with Egesta, Rhegion, and Leontinoi were only first steps in the right direction.

Pericles opposed the wilder manifestations of the *Drang nach Westen,* as he opposed any policy, however popular, that he deemed unsound or ill-timed; and so far he had been successful. He declined to register alarm or displeasure when the colony at Thouria turned its back on Athens, proclaiming the god Apollo as its "Founder," or when Syracuse in the early 'thirties planned to develop her land forces, and to increase her navy by 100 new triremes. The old alliances with Rhegion and Leontinoi were sufficient guarantees that Athens *could* intervene in the west, if need arose.

Athens, in Pericles' view if not in Kleon's, was, in the language of the 1930's, a sated power. As for potential enemies, the Peloponnesian League had made no move in 440 in support of Samos, and its chief naval power, Corinth, claimed credit at Athens for his non-intervention. Nothing important had changed between 439 and 435; and yet in 435 began a chain of events leading to a war which ultimately crippled the growing power of the Hellenic world. How this came to pass is a question still debated by historians, although we have one good first-hand authority—Thucydides—and, a point even more conducive to unanimity, only one.

Thucydides gives a lucid account of the events leading up to the war, but opines that behind them, as the "truest cause," lay Sparta's fear of the growing power of Athens. This sounds reasonable; and yet Athens, *pace* Thucydides, was surely *not* so powerful now as before the Egyptian disaster; and if Sparta moved in 432, why not in 440? Also, Thucydides' own narrative shows us a reluctant Sparta being badgered into war by Corinth, herself so recently pacific.

No responsible Athenian, Spartan, or Corinthian, it is

quite clear, wanted a general war, though some irresponsible people were not unwilling. (As Thucydides grimly says, there had been no war for some time, so there were plenty of young men.) But the war came, and during the last negotiations Pericles himself urged Athens to refuse concessions. How did this come about?

The answer seems to be, through fear: in diplomatic language, through the incompatible views of the Greek powers as to what was necessary for their security. Thucydides' account of Athens' reasons for taking the step that brought her into conflict with Corinth is that the Athenians (he does not actually say Pericles) considered that there was going to be another war with the Peloponnesians anyhow, and that, this being so, they wished to weaken potentially hostile navies and *to secure a good position* (the island of Corfu) *on the way to Italy and Sicily.*

At the back of Athens'—that is, of Pericles'—mind, then, was the west; and we must consider why.

The Thirty Years' Peace had left Greece divided indeed, but with a fairly stable balance of power, between the Delian and Peloponnesian Leagues, the whale and the elephant. But outside the Greek and Ægean world lay that Greek New World in Italy and Sicily, with its teeming cities, many of them larger, though politically less stable, than any in old Greece except Athens herself; a New World which if united on either side—in alliance with Athens, or under Dorian Syracuse, friendly to Corinth and Sparta—might seriously upset the balance of the Old.

Economic motives were present only in the background, though not less real on that account. Corinth did *not* urge Sparta to war because Athenian trade was penetrating the west; it had been doing that for a century. Nor is there any reason to think that Kleon and his fellow-tradesmen, interested in the west though they were, desired to crush by armed force a not very formidable rival. The economic background of the mutual anxieties lay farther back than that. Some of the Peloponnesian states, Thucydides shows us, required some imported corn; and they got much of it from the west, paying largely in Corinthian manufactures, eastern re-exports, services (e.g. Arcadian mercenaries), and tourist traffic (Olympia). Athens had no reason to desire to cut off these supplies in peace-time; but the fear that she might be able to probably preyed on many Corinthians' minds. At the same time, many at Athens, including Pericles, were increasingly conscious that their Empire—for all the glamour of Athens, and for all Athens had done to impose democracy—was held down, in the last analysis, by force. Idealists like Pericles hoped that the hankering after old autonomies was temporary; "realists" like Kleon probably reckoned that it was permanent, a "law of nature." Some simple people may have been unaware that it existed; but the politicians knew. This being so, the Athenians' feeling of security, that is their confidence of continued freedom from want and from revenge by enemies, depended on their navy. That navy exceeded in numbers (and vastly excelled in quality) all the other navies of Old Greece; the Long Walls were impregnable; and so Athens felt safe; but if the naval strength and immense ship-building capacity of the west were thrown into the scale, she would feel safe no longer. Hence the alliances with Leontinoi, Rhegion, and Egesta. Pericles' policy was a peace policy, but he kept a "foot in the door." The Peloponnesians did, in fact, when war came, propose to use their Sicilian allies for a prodigious building programme—up to a total of 500 triremes. (Athens' total strength, first line and reserve, was 300, plus 100 from Chios and Mytilene.) But nothing came of the scheme, and the strategy bequeathed by Pericles to his successors, of supporting the anti-Syracusan bloc with modest forces, proved quite sufficient to keep Syracuse employed. It was not till fourteen years after Pericles' death that Athens, under the reckless leadership of Alkibiades, made a serious effort to conquer the west; and then the Peloponnesian reaction was vigorous, and disastrous to Athens.

In 435, then, neither Athens nor the Peloponnesians wanted war, and neither was, in fact, trying to mobilise the west against the other; but there was mutual mistrust. When therefore in 433 Corinth, with her long-standing interests in the north-west of Greece proper, took action which appeared to Pericles likely to change the balance of naval power and the position on the western route, Pericles advised Athens to offer unyielding opposition. Corinth now in turn felt herself menaced with "encirclement," and succeeded in convincing Sparta and her other allies that the restless and aggressive Athenian democracy was a menace to them all.

The Greek state that was to play the part of "bleeding Kansas" in this rivalry for the west, Kerkyra or Korkyra (Corfu), was an ancient colony of Corinth, founded, it was said, at the same time as Syracuse and before the nearer colonies of Leukas and Ambrakia; but subsequent relations with the mother city had been bitter. Corinth, unlike most Greek states, had kept her nearer colonies dependent, and even sent out annual governors to them. In distant Syracuse Corinth had never attempted such a step, and Syracuse remained independent and friendly. But at Kerkyra, in the intermediate position, Corinth tried, and failed. The result had been wars of independence, separation, and bitter animosity.

Kerkyra, with her spacious and beautiful island territory, ample rainfall, and position of the coasting route to Italy, had prospered exceedingly, and was now the second naval power in Greece; she could raise at a pinch 120 triremes. She had always avoided entangling alliances; but Corinth had not forgotten, nor forgiven.

Farther up the Illyrian coast, by modern Durazzo, lay the colony of Epidamnos, planted by Kerkyra probably when subject to the great tyrants of Corinth, the house of Kypselos; the official founder, agreeably to ancient etiquette, had been a Corinthian. In or before 435, Epidamnos had a revolution: the people drove out their aristocracy, and the latter made common cause with the neighbouring Illyrians and began a guerilla war on the city by land and sea. The democrats, finding themselves hard pressed, appealed to Kerkyra; but though their envoys took the solemn step of casting themselves as suppliants before the altars of the city, Kerkyra declined to help them. The Kerkyraians do not appear to have been an amiable people.

The Epidamnians now (after consulting Delphi, which was proper form) threw themselves on the mercy of Corinth, as being also, in a way, their mother-city. The Corinthians accepted the protectorate, gladly, from every point of view; for economic reasons and also, not least, out of willingness to annoy Kerkyra; and they sent a force of volunteers from Corinth, Leukas, and Ambrakia, who, going chiefly by land, by what is now the Arta-Jannina-Valona route, "for fear of the Kerkyraians," reinforced Epidamnos.

And then Kerkyra did intervene. The Epidamnian exiles had been there with a counter-embassy, and by appealing to old family ties with the leading men of Kerkyra they met with more success. Having no desire to see Corinthian influence established so far north, the Kerkyraians peremptorily ordered the new settlers to leave Epidamnos, and meeting with a refusal, sat down to besiege it.

Corinth then mobilised in earnest. In addition to her own navy and those of her colonies, she called for assistance from her allies. Ships and men came from Megara and Epidauros, Troizen and Hermione, and economic assistance also from Thebes and Elis. The shock-waves spreading outwards from the trouble at Epidamnos were now reaching a wide area. Sparta began to take notice, and, anxious to check a dispute which might have unpredictable consequences, gave her support to Kerkyraian ambassadors at Corinth. They called upon Corinth to withdraw her troops and settlers from Epidamnos as being outside her proper sphere of influence, and offered to submit the whole dispute to the Delphic Oracle or to neutral arbitration. Otherwise, said the Kerkyraians, if menaced by a coalition, they would have to change their policy and seek allies where they could. This could only mean an appeal to Athens.

Corinth, however, demanded that Kerkyra should first withdraw her troops from Epidamnos. Kerkyra refused, but proposed a local armistice; the Corinthians refused in turn, sent a herald with a formal declaration of war, and put to sea with seventy-five triremes.

It was a fatal miscalculation. Kerkyra had a larger navy than Corinth, and launching every available ship, some of them old, met the allies with eighty galleys, while forty more kept up the blockade of Epidamnos. Off Leukimme, the south cape of Kerkyra, the islanders won a complete victory. They followed it up with a fierce naval offensive, harrying the coasts of Leukas until Corinth was forced to maintain garrisons there, and burning Kyllene, the naval port of Elis, which had lent ships to the expedition. On the very day of the battle, it is said, Epidamnos capitulated; the Kerkyraians kept the Corinthian settlers as prisoners and hostages, and sold the rest as slaves.

This was the end of the revolution at Epidamnos; but by this time the original cause of the dispute was no longer the vital point. Corinth settled herself grimly to prepare an overwhelming force. For two years her shipyards worked, till she had ninety triremes, the largest fleet that Corinth ever sent to sea. Her colonies and allies raised sixty more. Her crews were supplemented with hired rowers from abroad, largely from the allies of Athens. So far, it is noteworthy, both Athens and Sparta had remained strictly neutral, Sparta using her diplomacy to restrain Corinth, and Athens allowing her "allies" to enlist in the Corinthian service. In view of Athens' later behaviour, one may suspect that many Athenians were not unwilling to see the pressure on Kerkyra increased, calculating accurately what the result would be.

At Kerkyra men watched with increasing alarm the growth of Corinth's armaments. They could not, it appears, increase their own naval strength, probably because their isolation and unpopularity prevented them from hiring foreign crews. Their rowers, unlike those of Athens, were largely slaves; but only citizens of Kerkyra could be trusted to fight on deck. As the Corinthian build-up proceeded, they realised that their cherished isolation would no longer serve. In 433, an embassy from Kerkyra set sail for Athens.

The Corinthians soon heard of this move, and sent a

counter-delegation; and Thucydides gives a detailed summary of the debate that resulted. The Corinthians urged their own recent correct and friendly behaviour, and the desirability of furthering the recent *détente* between the states; the Kerkyraians, the strategic advantages of the alliance which they could offer, in view of what one of them called "Sparta's desire for war through fear of Athens, Corinth's influence with Sparta and hostility to you, and their desire to secure Kerkyra as a preliminary to operations against you."

These assertions about Corinth and Sparta were, as we have seen, not borne out by those states' recent conduct, and when, after hearing both sides, the Assembly stood adjourned, public opinion was, on the whole, for refusing to intervene; but next day, after the speakers of Athens had been heard, there was a change of feeling. The speakers argued that *in view of the probability of another war anyhow,* the prospective enemy must not be allowed to secure Kerkyra. So the decisive step was taken; Athens made with Kerkyra, not a full alliance—for under that, Kerkyra could have demanded a joint offensive against Corinth, contrary to the treaty of 445—but a defensive alliance only; and a modest "token" squadron of ten ships —a warning, not a threat—was ordered to Kerkyra. The general selected, too, was one anxious to avoid war with the Peloponnese: Lakedaimonios, son of Kimon, whose name means "Spartan," and whom Pericles had once twitted with being more Spartan that Athenian, even in name.

But Pericles knew well that the die had been cast. It may have been from this Kerkyra debate, or later, that his saying is quoted: "I see as it were a cloud of war rising from the Peloponnese." The expression "war-cloud" was a new metaphor then. From this time on, the cloud continued to rise, relentlessly, till it covered the sky.

The Corinthians' blood was up, and they were no longer acting on a basis of cold calculation. It soon became clear that ten ships under a son of Kimon were not going to deter them, and Athens sent twenty more, under Glaukon (Xanthippos' brother-in-law) and Drakontides, who though a colleague of Pericles was no friend of his. Thirty good Athenian ships, plus the navy of Kerkyra, should be sufficient to ensure that Corinth could not gain a victory. It would have been almost as easy to send sixty ships, or a hundred, but (apart from expense) the Assembly was acting on the calculation, explicitly thrashed out in the debate, that it was good policy to let other navies fight each other, in order to weaken them.

The twenty ships left Piræus on their long voyage round the Peloponnese, only just in time. They had, in fact, not reached Kerkyra when the enemy were reported approaching the island, and the Kerkyraians with the ten Athenian ships, which were under orders to avoid actual fighting unless the enemy attempted a landing, put out against them. There was severe, protracted, and bloody fighting between the two great fleets of galleys, their decks crowded with archers and armoured soldiers. The Athenians noted with contempt that there had been no move, in these Dorian navies, to reduce the number of "passengers" and manœuvre for an attack with the ram in the "modern" style.

Gradually numbers told, especially as the Kerkyraian left wing, which defeated Corinth's allies, wasted time in a long pursuit. Two-thirds of Kerkyra's navy were being overwhelmed; "and the Athenians, seeing the Kerkyraians hard pressed, began to intervene more unreservedly. At first they held off to the extent of not actually ramming; but when the rout was becoming plain to see and the Corinthians were pressing on, then, indeed, it was all hands to the work, and there were no more distinctions; and so it came to this, that Corinthians and Athenians lifted their hands against each other." First blood had been shed in the Peloponnesian War.

Meanwhile the twenty ships under Glaukon and Drakontides were coming up from Kephallenia at cruising speed, knowing nothing of what was taking place, but timing their journey to reach Kerkyra by nightfall. At the moment when they sighted the island, the Corinthians, having reformed, were about to attack again, while the remnants of the defending fleet were preparing for a desperate resistance against an attempted landing. "It was late evening," continues Thucydides, "and men had raised the battle-hymn, ready to engage, when the Corinthians suddenly backed water. They had seen twenty Athenian ships coming up . . . and suspected that there were more. Thus the battle ended at nightfall, and the twenty ships sailed in, through the corpses and wreckage . . . and came to land."

So narrowly did Kerkyra escape disaster.

Next morning the whole thirty Athenian ships and what was left of their allies sailed across to the Corinthian anchorage and offered battle; but the Corinthians, with many ships damaged and no facilities for repair, had no stomach for it. They stood on the defensive close inshore, and sent over a cutter to protest, without a herald's staff (the customary "flag of truce") in token that they did not recognise a state of war as existing with Athens. . . . The Athenians replied that they were not starting a war, nor contravening the Thirty Years' Peace, but they were defending their allies. If the Corinthians desired to sail home, or anywhere else but against Kerkyra, the sea was open.

Angry and humiliated, the Corinthians went.

Chapter 12

Peace or War?

SPARTA HAD SHOWN that she disapproved of Corinth's adventure in the north-west; but the Athenian alliance with Kerkyra had alarmed Peloponnesian opinion, and a war-party was growing. Pericles used the respite in making ready for what he was sure must come.

It has been believed by many moderns, following a theory mentioned with reserve by Plutarch, that Pericles provoked the Peloponnesian War in order to restore his own position, shaken by the attacks on his friends (all, according to Plutarch, in quick succession), and by a threatened attack on his own administration of finance. Alkibiades, hearing that his guardian was too busy to see him one day because he was working out "how to give his accounts to the people," is said to have commented: "He'd do better to work out how *not* to give them." The remark sounds likely enough, but that Pericles took the hint is a large assumption. In fact, the attacks on his friends may have been spread over many years, and the attack on his accounts have taken place during the war (see pp. 116-18, 157, and 199). Thucydides makes it quite clear that Pericles, at the beginning of the war and just before it, was as much the acknowledged leader of Athens as he had ever been.

Nevertheless, Pericles did advise the Assembly against concessions; potential enemies must not control Corfu and the way to the west; but it is also likely that personal motives weighed with him, at least to the extent that he was convinced that he could save Athens (especially from her own great fault of over-confidence) and that no one else could; which was only too true. If, then, there was to be a war—one more war, to confirm Athens' new order—it had better be soon, while he, Pericles, already over sixty, was there to lead it. Pericles the Alkmeonid was a politician and a lover of power, in spite of the Parthenon.

Pericles and his associates used the last years of peace to prepare for war. Probably in the civil year 434-433, the state finances were reorganised under two detailed decrees, proposed by a certain Kallias. The name is a common one, but the proposer was probably a leading general of this time, son of Kalliades, a name also current in the great family of the Heralds. Under one of these Acts, which were both passed on one day, it is provided that after the completion of a reserve fund of 3,000 talents in Athenian coined money, deposited in the Treasury of Athene (evidently under an earlier Act), debts to the other gods shall be paid off. (Athens had probably borrowed from temple treasuries to finance the building programme, especially before the battle over the use of League funds was won.) To this end are to be applied the surpluses both of League and internal revenue. A new body of Treasurers of the Other Gods, parallel to the existing Treasurers of Athene, is established to take joint charge of both funds, which are all to be stored in the closed Back Chamber of the Parthenon. Finally, when all outstanding debts have been paid, surplus funds shall be added to those available for maintenance of the walls and the naval arsenal.

Under the second decree it is directed that the Propylaia and certain other works on the Acropolis be "finished off," under plans provided by the architect (Mnesikles?). Ten talents a year are provided for maintenance and repairs; and it is forbidden under heavy penalties to make any other payment exceeding 10,000 drachmas (1⅔ talents) from Athene's treasury except for urgent repairs, without a special vote of indemnity from the Assembly. This was the regular method of safe-guarding a reserve fund.

Thus under the first decree Athens was provided with two reserve funds (when war broke out, Pericles was able to announce that they amounted to 6,000 talents); and under the second the great building programme was wound up and a policy of retrenchment on peace expenditure introduced. The completion of Mnesikles' original design for the two great wings of the Propylaia would have to wait for a more propitious time. But that time never came.

It was probably the same Kallias who, in the new civil year which began at midsummer 433, formally proposed the decree renewing the western alliances with Leontinoi and Rhegion. He must have been one of Pericles' leading lieutenants; but his fame was brief. He was killed in action in 432, while commanding the Athenian forces operating against Poteidaia—a Corinthian colony which was also a member-state of the Delian League, and which at this juncture revolted with the active support of a volunteer brigade from its mother-city.

In 432, then, Athenian and Corinthian troops (with other Peloponnesian mercenaries) had met in a pitched battle before Poteidaia, and Kallias' army, less its commander and 150 more Athenians, was besieging a leading Corinthian general in that city. Also, before Poteidaia openly revolted, its government had sent secret emissaries to Sparta; and Sparta—that is to say, some or all of the ephors, the annual magistrates for the year—had promised, if Athens used force against Poteidaia, to intervene in arms; striking evidence of a change in feeling since the Corfu episode. Sparta was not unanimous for war even now. The old King Archidamos, who knew what war with Athens would mean, headed the peace party. But Pericles, having decided that war, or at least a show-down and trial of strength, was now inevitable, took his own measures. At this very moment, when all was in the balance, Athens took economic sanctions against another of Sparta's allies—Megara. Accusing the Megarians of having sinned against the gods by ploughing up sacred land (the sort of excuse that was common form when one intended to pick a quarrel), she excluded all Megarian trade from the harbours and markets of the Empire, by what came to be known as the Megarian Decree.

Athens had not forgotten how the Megarians in 446 had massacred their Athenian garrison—a garrison which

they themselves had called in twelve years earlier to save
them from Corinth. Relations had no doubt been bad
ever since, but we know nothing of them. To this small,
densely populated, eastward-trading state, which had
specialised in textile manufactures for export, the decree
meant slow starvation. This naturally added Megara's
voice to the outcry already being raised at Sparta by
Corinth.

Other if less serious complaints against Athens multi-
plied. The people of Aigina complained, through secret
emissaries, that Athens was interfering in their internal
affairs, contrary to the promise of "autonomy" in the
treaty of 445. Athens, as we have seen, was constantly
infringing her allies' autonomy in practice, either on
grounds of security or of economic expediency. The ukase
that states of the League were not to trade with Megara
was such an infringement in itself.

In these circumstances Sparta invited delegates from
her allies to address the Spartan Assembly on the Athenian question. Corinthian envoys had been canvassing
vigorously for a twelvemonth; and delegate after delegate
rose to complain of Athens as a bad neighbour and a
danger to all. After letting others work upon Spartan
feelings, as part of a prearranged plan, the Corinthian
spokesman rose last to sum up the common grievances;
and Thucydides puts into his mouth a vivid picture of the
sanguine, restless, and daring Athenian character, which
had accomplished so much and roused such bitter hatred
and fear.

It now remained for the Spartans, without the presence
of strangers, to consider whether the pressure to be exerted
on Athens should be carried to the point of an early
declaration of war or not. But there was one further intervention. Some Athenian envoys happened, Thucydides
says, to be in Sparta on other business, and they asked
permission to address the meeting. It was granted, and
an Athenian spokesman came forward.

The speech that follows is an extraordinary performance. It is reasonable to consider its main lines to be
those of a speech actually made, not a free composition

by Thucydides, for the reasons that: (1) Thucydides as a rising politician had every opportunity of hearing about it; (2) it is emphatically *not* the speech on "the case for Athens" that one would expect; and (3) Thucydides tells us, *not* in the speech, that the ambassadors decided not to reply to the specific charges against Athens, but simply to advise the Spartans to take care.

The whole speech is, in fact, truculent, arrogant, and provocative. "In view of all this outcry against us we propose, not to answer the charges (you are not our judges) but to warn you against being persuaded into an imprudent decision on a serious issue. . . . It is necessary to mention our services in the Persian Wars, however tired people may be of our continually referring to them." [Mention of Marathon, Salamis, Themistocles, et cetera, duly follows.] "You Spartans let us down by your slowness, but we saved you all the same. . . . We gained our empire, not by conquest, but because you backed out of continuing the war against Persia, and the allies themselves asked us to take the lead. . . . Naturally later, when feeling was turning against us and there had been some attempted secessions, we could not lay down our power. . . . It is an eternal law that the weaker is ruled by the stronger. . . . We deserve our position (you thought so too until it suited you to start talking about justice). . . . We are in fact fairer than most people would be in our position . . . and as a direct result the allies grumble, because in self-defence we have transferred some commercial lawsuits from the Empire to our own perfectly fair courts at Athens, instead of considering how other people treat their subjects; how the Persians, for example, treated them themselves. . . . If *you* should ever demolish us and succeed to our position, you will soon lose your present popularity, if you behave as you did in the Persian Wars; for the Spartan code at home is unlike anyone else's, but when you go abroad you do not abide by either that or the common customs of Greece." The speaker ends with a patronising warning that war is a chancy business; Sparta had better be careful.

What, one may well ask, could any intelligent Athenian

expect to be the effect of such a speech at such a moment?
What its effect was appears in the sequel.

The Spartans debated by themselves. Speaker after
speaker gave his opinion, mostly for war. At last came
forward the veteran King Archidamos, to plead for caution. Sparta was not ready for war; not with the great
maritime and financial power of Athens. This would be a
long war, a very different matter from a land campaign
inside the Peloponnese. Athens could only be brought
down by subverting her allies; and the Peloponnesian
League was too weak at sea even to relieve any cities
which did revolt. The only damage that Sparta could do
Athens was to devastate her territory. It was most unlikely that this would bring Athens to her knees, and consequently it was sound strategy *not* to resort to this step
at once, but to keep it as a threat—like a hostage, who
could only be killed once. Athens had already expressed
her willingness to submit to arbitration the question
whether any of her proceedings contravened the Treaty
of 445. Sparta should make representations, certainly,
and back them with preparations for war; but there should
be no ultimatum yet.

But his counsel fell upon deaf ears. The next speaker
was the Ephor presiding over the Assembly, in person;
and he harked straight back to the speech of the Athenian. He had failed to follow this long oration, he said
(a favourite gambit with Spartans, who prided themselves
on their "laconic," i.e. Lakonian, brevity). The Athenians
had praised themselves at great length, but they had not
shown that they were not wronging Sparta's allies. "Others
may have maritime and financial power, but we have
loyal allies and must not betray them." Hesitation would
better befit the intending aggressor than the defender.
And with that he called for a vote "worthy of Sparta,"
and using his powers as presiding officer, that no voice
might be heard after his, put the question to the vote: Did
Sparta consider that the Athenians had broken the Treaty?
Not content with the usual primitive Spartan method of
voting by acclamation, he called for a division.

There was a large majority for war.

It is clear that the unnamed Athenian's speech had contributed not a little to this result; but we have still not answered the question—what did the Athenian envoys *expect* of such a speech? That Athenian ambassadors were so obtuse as not to realise what the effect would be is almost unthinkable; but the only alternative is that the speech was a piece of deliberate sabotage at the outset of the "peace or war" negotiations. It is scarcely likely that the ambassadors ventured on such a step on their own initiative; and so one is almost forced to the conclusion that their "accidental" presence at Sparta was no accident at all; that the leading men of Athens—that is to say, that Pericles—hearing of the proposed congress at Sparta, had made an excuse to send an embassy "on other matters," privately briefed to take the line that they took.

Here, as in the Megarian Decree and in Pericles' whole attitude to the crisis, we find evidence of his consistent attitude, that if war must come it had better come while he was there to control it; no war of annihilation, a war, in fact, with as little bloodshed as might be; a strictly limited war, which would show the Peloponnesian hotheads that their spears were impotent against the walls of Athens, and that Athens could hit back at sea, with stinging pinpricks on the coasts of Lakonia and with ruinous effect against Corinth and Megara. In a few years, at latest, the enemy's impetus would be exhausted. The land of Attica would suffer; but the Peloponnesians, the one solid combination in the Greek world outside Athens' own empire, would retire with irretrievable loss of prestige, hopelessly baffled in a war of their own choosing. Even before that, Megara might well have been starved into surrender. After it, sure as fate, disintegration would commence.

And then, perhaps, who knows? Perhaps at last the general Greek federation, and the Athenian peace?

Sparta was committed, but though the Corinthians clamoured for speedy action to save Poteidaia, King Archidamos was in no hurry. The influential peace-party still worked hard for delay, hoping against hope that Athens would make some concessions before, in the Greek phrase, "anything irremediable had happened."

Sparta had still to call a further congress of allied delegates; this time of plenipotentiaries to vote on whether they endorsed Sparta's decision that Athens had broken the Treaty. To the accompaniment of further Corinthian lobbying, they voted for war ("A war to win a stable peace," said the Corinthians); but even now there was no campaign in 432. Preparations were set on foot for the spring; and meanwhile there was much coming and going of Spartan embassies to Athens.

The first demand was that Athens should expel the Accursed of the Goddess—a reference to the Curse of the Alkmeonidai, which was almost exactly two hundred years old that year. The reason for this demand, apart from its being common form to choose a religious pretext when one intended to pick a quarrel, was of course to strike at Pericles, "from the opinion," says Thucydides, "that if he were banished Athens would be easier to deal with. They had not much hope of achieving this actual result, but hoped to injure his popularity by rousing the feeling that the war was going to be largely about him. For"—adds Thucydides, in a sentence fatal to the theory that Pericles' position was seriously shaken—" he was the most powerful man of his generation, and in his leadership of the state he opposed the Spartans at every point, and was against concessions, urging the Athenians to war." The transparent attack on him was a complete failure, merely increasing, if that were possible, his prestige. The Athenians merely replied by calling upon Sparta to expel those tainted by two breaches of sanctuary (both at the expense of revolutionaries) in the last fifty years.

But Sparta had also more serious and mundane demands to make: that Athens should call off the blockade of Poteidaia, grant Aigina her autonomy, and—with special emphasis—revoke the Megarian Decree. There was no mention of the original cause of trouble, Kerkyra. It was too obvious that Athens was committing no breach of the Treaty of 445 in concluding a defensive alliance with a neutral state. The Megarian Decree was the action which could be most clearly construed as aggression; and the ambassador Polyalkes stated most explicitly that if it were repealed there would be no war. Pericles politely explained that the Assembly had just passed one of its favourite "safeguarding" acts, forbidding under penalties the removal of the Decree, which had been, by order, inscribed on bronze and set up on the Acropolis. "Well, then, turn its face to the wall," urged Polyalkes; "there's no law against that." He won some repute by this witticism; but he made no impression upon Pericles. As Pericles saw it, neither the Megarian Decree nor any other concession could any longer be considered in isolation. To submit to arbitration on the question whether Athens was contravening the Treaty—a very arguable point—was one thing; to make concessions to demands backed by the threat of war was quite another. The real question at issue was already that which arises in war: which of two contending parties was to impose its will upon the other.

Sparta's last word was: "Sparta wishes the peace to continue, and continue it can if you will leave the Greeks their freedom"; and on this ultimatum the issue was laid before the Athenian Assembly. Opinions were divided, many feeling that the Megarian Decree was really not important enough to fight about; but at this point Pericles intervened in the debate.

The speech which Thucydides puts into his mouth is largely in Thucydides' own tortuous oratorical style—almost inevitably, since in Pericles' generation political speeches were not yet written down. But Thucydides must have heard it; and there is a distinction about this speech —a humour, and, in spite of Thucydides, almost a simplicity—which are not to be found in the speeches which Thucydides, on his own showing, made up according to his ideas of what was appropriate. This is especially marked in the passages that would naturally be best remembered by a listener, at the beginning and end. It is reasonable to suppose, then, that we have here Thucydides' faithful recollection of Pericles, speech on the ultimatum.

"I hold to my former opinion, Athenians," began Pericles, "that we should not yield to the Peloponnesians; and I do so although I know very well that people do not feel at all the same during a war as they do when they are persuaded to go into it; they change their minds with their fortunes. But I see it as my duty to give you now the same advice as before; and, I beg you, in the name of justice, to stand by what we resolve on together, even if we meet with hard times; for if you do not stick to your opinions, then you can hardly claim credit for them when they turn out well! Circumstances frequently behave just as unreasonably as people—which is why we customarily blame Fortune for anything that upsets our calculations."

After this appeal to the people not to turn against their leaders if there were hard times ahead, Pericles accused the enemy of conspiring against Athens: "For the Treaty provides that each side shall hold what they then had, and that differences be submitted to arbitration; but they have made no proposal for arbitration to us, nor accepted the proposal when we made it. They *want* to settle the dispute by war and not by argument, and their present approach is not a complaint but an order. . . . Let none of you think that we shall be fighting about a little thing if we refuse to repeal the Megarian Decree, of which they say that if we repeal it there will be no war, nor blame yourselves hereafter as having gone to war for a trifle, for this 'little thing' includes a supreme test of your resolution. If you give way, some more serious demand will follow, on the calculation that your first concession shows that you are afraid.[1] Make up your minds, then, either to submit before you get hurt, or that if we are to fight, as I say we must, then we will not give way either on great or little

[1] Cf. the remarks in *Mein Kampf* on the psychology of making demand after demand, backed by threats of war—because people who have yielded a point that leaves them weaker, rather than fight, will go on yielding—feeling progressively less and less inclined to fight, with what remains of their strength, for what remains of their freedom. How admirably Pericles would have seen through Hitler!

matters, nor will we hold our possessions on sufferance; for any demand, great or small, made as an order, without an attempt at legal settlement, has the same meaning —slavery."

Pericles went on to argue that Athens had every reason to hope for victory. (One wonders if Thucydides has thrown in a few details from later war speeches.) The Peloponnesian League has a rudimentary organisation and no unified organs of government; the states have not even identical interests. Above all, the enemy are weak economically and financially. Peasant farmers, such as they are, are always readier for personal than for financial sacrifice. They have no reserve funds, and will often be unable to seize their chances, because they will have to scratch up money before they can launch an expedition; and "chances in war will not wait." As for their raising a navy, the idea need not be taken seriously. "You yourselves have been sailors since the Persian Wars, and you are learning still. A navy is a highly technical service and cannot be improvised."

Next he outlined the strategy to be adopted. Attica was not an island, more's the pity; well: "We must behave as nearly as possible as if it were, by abandoning our land and farms, and holding firmly the city and the sea." They must not let themselves be stung into fighting a pitched battle against superior numbers to save their land, because even a victory would not be decisive, and a defeat would: "It would lose us, in addition, the empire, the source of our strength; for the allies will not stay quiet if we are not in a condition for operations against them." (We are a long way now from the days when Athens could employ League troops against Spartans.) "So," he goes on, "you must keep your pity, not for property but for the manpower that wins it. Indeed, if I thought there was a chance of persuading you, I would urge you to go out and devastate your own land now, to show the Peloponnesians that you are not going to submit for its sake!

"On every ground I am confident that we shall come through, if you will refrain from attempting new conquests during the war and from running any avoidable risks, for indeed, I am less afraid of the enemy's bright ideas than of our own bad ones. That, however, is a subject that will keep for another time, when the case arises; but now, let us send back these envoys with the answer that we will admit the Megarians to our markets and harbours if the Spartans will renounce in favour of us and our allies their practice of deporting aliens[2] (there is nothing about that in the Treaty, but nor is there about this); that we will grant autonomy to the Cities, if they had it when we made the Treaty, and if the Spartans will extend the principle of autonomy, in favour of their own allies, to include the free choice of their form of government, even if the Spartans do not like it; that we are ready to submit to arbitration under the treaty, and that we will not start a war—but if we are attacked, we will defend ourselves. . . ."

The Assembly supported Pericles by a large majority. But the poet Euripides, with an ache in his heart, finished off his *Mêdeia* for the next spring festival. There was in it a choral lyric on Athens and Attica, on the lovely rivulet Kephisos and the "holy, unravaged land"—that land which, as Athenians were proud to boast, had never been harried by foemen in living memory "except for the Persian War."

The winter passed relentlessly, enlivened by the coming and going of missions between states and the sound of hammering in shipyards and in armourers' shops; and with the spring two-thirds of every Peloponnesian ally's military strength was concentrated at Corinth for an invasion of Attica. The army was in high spirits. They were the best fighting-men of Greece, they were in superior numbers, and they were marching to liberate Greece from the tyranny of Athens. Old Archidamos, who had led Spartan armies to victory before most of his young spearmen were born, thought it desirable to warn them that Athens would prove a tough and resourceful enemy, and

[2] As they did periodically, for military security reasons.

that the carelessness born of over-confidence was the best possible way to invite regrettable incidents.

He then sent forward Melesippos, one of the late ambassadors, in a last effort to obtain some concession that would give him an excuse for going no farther; but the Athenians turned him back outside the city. Pericles had carried a resolution that any further envoys should be sent back with the answer that if the Peloponnesians wished for any more negotiations, they should first demobilise. They sent an escort with Melesippos, to see that he held no communication with anybody. They left him on the frontier, and Melesippos went on his way with the parting words: "This day will be the beginning of great evils for Greece."

Chapter 13

The Faith of a Democrat

ARCHIDAMOS WITH A HEAVY HEART gave the order to advance. Even now, on reaching Megara, he took not the direct coast road by Eleusis, but the mountain tracks into north-western Attica, where he besieged the frontier fort of Oinoe on the road to Thebes. He thus cleared the wooded hill-country out of which a resourceful enemy might have harassed his marching columns strung out on the narrow coast road. Also, having no cavalry of any kind, he wished to make contact with his Boiotian allies, needing their horsemen to face those of Athens (reinforced from Thessaly) before letting loose his infantry to forage and devastate. But Archidamos certainly took his time over all this, undeterred by the grumbling of his army, who complained that they were losing good loot by his "pro-Athenian" and "cowardly" action, giving the enemy time to evacuate their farms. He was holding to his policy of not "killing the only hostage" till the last possible moment. If only Pericles would make some pacific move!

Meanwhile the evacuation of Attica was in full swing. Cattle and sheep were ferried over to Euboia or Salamis, women and children and household gear were sent into Athens—even to the woodwork of many of the country houses; an interesting sidelight on the standard of Attic country life. People in outlying districts, no doubt, stored their goods in the other walled places, such as Eleusis or Rhamnous. Pericles had had his way.

The fact that it was necessary did not make the evacuation any less unpleasant. The corn was in the ear, and the weather just turning hot; it was the season when modern Athenians move out of town, not in. The long streams of refugees moved along the dusty tracks, carrying what they could of their possessions in wagons or on mules and donkeys or, the poorest of them, in heavy bundles on their own backs; with the likelihood that anything left behind, unless carefully hidden, would be plundered or destroyed.

At Athens, there was no reception or billeting scheme, though Plutarch seems to imply that relief in money was issued to the distressed. For country people to take refuge within the walls was usual in Greece when there were enemies about, though it had never been done on such a scale. The usual procedure was that one went to stay with relations; but in Attica—much more of a "country" than the territories of most Greek states—many of the peasant families had no connections in town, and camped wherever they could; some in stifling little improvised shacks, some in the towers of the fortifications, many in the temples and shrines of gods and heroes "except those of the Acropolis, and any others that were securely locked up"—just as an even larger and more pitiful throng of "displaced persons" camped in Greek churches and built shacks around the Acropolis after the Asia Minor disaster. Later they spread gradually all along the five miles of the Long Walls to Piræus. A modern doctor would have been alarmed at the danger to health, especially as there was a plague raging in Egypt and parts of Asia, with which Athens was still trading. But the peasants of Attica were a healthy stock, and there were no ill effects this year.

Pericles encouraged the will to resist with another war speech, containing little rhetoric, but—much better at such a time of general discomfort—plenty of cheering and reassuring facts; a general summary of Athens' armed and financial strength. The army included 13,000 "first-line" armoured infantry, besides as many more for garrison duty, found by the older men and the young "cadets"; 3,000 armoured infantry of the Resident Foreigners were also usually employed for defence only. (This great number of 16,000 armoured men merely for "holding the line" is accounted for by the length of the perimeter, Athens—Piræus—Pháleron, nearly seventeen miles, and

the garrisons in the other walled towns and border forts.)
Athens had also 1,200 cavalry, including the mounted
archers, and 1,600 foot archers; the navy had 300 triremes
ready for service. As Archidamos had warned his people,
no other single city had anything like such manpower.
Financially, the state had 6,000 talents in coined silver
deposited on the Acropolis, and 600 talents a year coming
in from the Empire.[1] Athens should win, repeated Pericles, if she held to the sound strategy of avoiding a land
battle and keeping the subject allies well in hand. "It is
sound planning and economic strength," said he, "that decide most issues in war."

He added that Archidamos was an old friend of his,
but that that should not harm the state, and that if, in the
coming invasion, Archidamos should protect his lands
from devastation, he would make them over to the Treasury. Pericles privately felt that there was quite a chance
that this might happen, either as an old-world courtesy on
Archidamos' part, or as a piece of "psychological war-
fare."

Archidamos at Oinoe was making no progress, his
spearmen being helpless, as usual, against strong stone
walls. Finally he gave it up and, with Boiotian cavalry in
the van, crossed the hills into the plain of Eleusis, where
devastation began in earnest. An Athenian cavalry force
was driven back east of Eleusis; but Archidamos declined
to follow up through the narrow pass where the Sacred
Way cuts through the Aigaleos Ridge. He took the more
northern route, followed by the modern railway, between
Aigaleos and Parnes, and so came in sight of Athens,
about seven miles away.

Before him lay the huge, straggling village of Acharnai,
the largest in population of all the "wards" of Attica; it
had probably grown recently out of all recognition, for its
charcoal burners, near the forests of Parnes, were now the

[1] The total *tribute*, as shown by the quota lists, some of which are
nearly complete, was under 400 talents; e.g. 388 talents for the
financial year 433-432. Evidently there were important other
sources of revenue in addition.

chief suppliers of fuel to the city. Here, if anywhere, by burning the houses of Athenians before their eyes, Archidamos hoped to provoke the enemy to battle.

At Athens the hope had survived till that very hour, even when the enemy were reported burning round Eleusis, that perhaps they would come no farther, but withdraw like Pleistoanax's army fifteen years before. But now the unthinkable was happening; Acharnai was in flames, the vines were being trampled down, Boiotian camp-followers were carrying off anything movable, and an enemy army stood there to cover the spoilers. All Pericles' sage advice was forgotten, and groups gathered in the streets disputing furiously, while oracle-mongers hawked their wares, varied to suit all tastes. Lead us out to battle, clamoured the Acharnians. There should have been no war, grumbled others. There were few who did not blame Pericles, on at least one ground or the other. Kleon the Tanner, the prophet of ruthlessness and of l'audace, makes his first appearance in our sources, in some typically bitter lines of Hermippos, about this time. Some expected a special meeting of the Assembly; but Pericles, never greater than in this hour, refused, fearing that the people, once convened, might take worse advice than his. Confident in the necessity of his plan, he declined to do more than send out cavalry to prevent small parties of marauders from coming down into the plain before the city; while, as a relief to men's feelings, preparations were pushed on for the great counter-raid by sea against the Peloponnese.

Another popular step, for which there was also a strategic reason, was taken a little later this year. The Athenians ejected the whole population of Aigina, and settled Athenians there as small-holders. It was a brutal measure, but the island's strategic position made it necessary; it lay too near the Peloponnesian coast, and a sudden raid might have transformed it again into an enemy outpost. As most of the quoted sayings of Pericles date from his later years, indeed, it may be that his phrase about the "eye-sore of Piræus" comes from the debate on this measure.

As the days passed Archidamos realised that his old friend's prudence had prevailed. There was still no fighting worth mentioning on land, except for a skirmish in which Thessalian as well as Athenian cavalry were encountered, at a place called Phrygia, "the Brushwood"; and from the foothills of Parnes one day he and all his host could see the gulf covered with white sails, as a hundred Athenian galleys, carrying four hundred archers and a thousand armoured men, set sail for Lakonia. Provisions, too, were running short; and after a week or two at Acharnai Archidamos marched away up the wide valley between Pentelikos and Parnes, burning as he went, as far as the Boiotian frontier, and so returned home through friendly territory.

The hundred Athenian ships, plus fifty from Kerkyra, raided the south and west coasts of the Peloponnese, won over the great island of Kephallenia, a useful stepping-stone, and captured Sollion, a small Corinthian colony in Akarnania; while thirty more under Kleopompos, the son of Kleinias (no doubt a kinsman of Alkibiades' family), harried Lokris, opposite Euboia. Finally, after the Peloponnesian army had gone home, Pericles led out the main army to work off their anger on the territory of hapless Megara, against whom Athens had now declared a truceless and relentless war.

So the campaign ended, after much burning but little loss of life, just as Pericles had predicted. It only remained, to Pericles' mind, to see how long this needed to go on before the enemy got tired of it. Next year the seaborne counter-offensive could be on a greater scale.

"That winter," says Thucydides, "the Athenians, following their ancestral custom, held a state funeral for the first men to fall in the war. The form of it is as follows. The bones" [after cremation soon after the battle] "are laid out in a tent two days before, and any who wish bring offerings to their own dead. Then, when the funeral takes place, large coffins of cypresswood are carried along on wagons, one for each tribe, containing the bones; and one empty bier is also carried, for the missing, whose bodies could not be recovered for burial. Anyone who wishes, citizen or stranger, joins in the procession, and the women-folk of the dead stand by the grave, wailing. They bury them in the public sepulchre, which is in the most beautiful approach to the city" [on the Sacred Way to Eleusis, outside the Dipylon Gate]; "it is there that they always bury those fallen in war, except the men of Marathon; they, out of respect to their special valour, were buried on the field. Then, when they have laid them in the earth, a man chosen by the city for his ability and reputation, speaks over them an appropriate eulogy; and after that they disperse. This custom they followed throughout the war, whenever the occasion arose.

"Over these first of the fallen, Pericles, the son of Xanthippos, was chosen to speak; so at the appropriate moment he came forward from the tomb, mounted a high platform which had been constructed so that he might be heard by as many of the crowd as possible, and spoke to the following effect."

What follows is the famous Funeral Oration, which, since Pericles (and Thucydides) made it the occasion for recording Pericles' political testament and confession of faith, is here translated almost in full. Being a war-time speech, it is full of digs at the enemy: at the Spartan peace-time security measures, for example, or, near the end, in the contrast of Athenian courage with that of the austere Spartans, whose lives, a Greek wag said, were made so miserable for them that it was no wonder they threw them away. But the most interesting part of it is Pericles' ideal picture of the Athenian democracy; and in this the most striking trait is perhaps the strong resemblance of its main lines to the hostile yet somehow loving accounts of Plato and of the Old Oligarch.

"Most men," said Pericles, as Thucydides remembered him, "who have spoken in this place have praised the legislator who added this speech to the proceedings. . . . For my part, I should have thought it sufficient that when men have proved themselves in action, by actions we should honour them, as we have now done in this public burial, instead of letting the credit of many brave men be at the mercy of one man's words, according as he speaks well or badly. . . . However, since our ancestors thought fit that this should be done, I must obey the law and try to speak not worse than you would desire and expect.

"I will speak first of our forefathers; for it is fit and right on such an occasion that we should honour their memory. They by their courage held this land generation after generation and were neither driven out nor enslaved. They deserve our praise; but still more our fathers, who added to their inheritance the empire that we now hold, and handed it on to us, not without labour. That empire we ourselves, those of us who are in middle life, have still further increased, and we have made our city the best able in the world to stand alone, whether in war or peace. But I do not propose to speak at length of the operations of war by which that power has been won and defended, either by us or our fathers, against foes barbarian or Greek. These are matters of which you know as well as I. Rather I will speak of the customs, the constitution and manner of life, under which we have reached these heights, and from this subject I will pass on to the praise of the Fallen; a subject not unfitting for this occasion, and one about which, for all this multitude of citizens and strangers, it is worth while to hear.

"Ours is a constitution which does not imitate those of our neighbours, but is rather a pattern to others. Because power rests with the majority and not with a few, it is called a democracy; in private disputes all are equal before the law, and in public life men are honoured for conspicuous achievement in any activity, and not for sectional reasons; nor is any poor man, who has it in him to do good service to the city, prevented by his obscurity. Ours is a free state, both in politics and in daily life; we do not resent it or bear a grudge against our neighbour if his amusements are not ours; for such resentments, though they may break no bones, remain unpleasant. Thus we are free and tolerant in our social life; yet at the same time we respect and obey the laws and lawful authorities; especially those laws that are for the protection of the weak, and those unwritten laws whose sanction is dishonour.

"We, best of all men, have provided ourselves with recreation for the mind, both in games and festivals at every season of the year, and in the beauty of our own belongings,[2] the delight in which, day by day, leaves no room for dreariness. And because of the greatness of our city, all the trade of the world flows in to her, and we can enjoy the products of distant lands as easily as our own.

"We are superior to our enemies, too, in our preparations for war. Our city is open to the world. *We* are not always expelling foreigners for fear of their learning or seeing something of military importance; for we trust not so much in secret armaments as in our native courage. In education, too, they try to inculcate manliness from youth up by a laborious training; *we* live freely, and yet we face the same dangers quite as readily as they. . . . But if we can do this—if we can rely, not on compulsion but on a tradition of bravery—so much the better for us. We do not exhaust ourselves with our preparations before the trouble arises, and yet when it comes we prove quite as brave as they who are always labouring.

"Here, then, we have cause to admire our city—and not in this alone: we are lovers also of beauty with simplicity, and of the things of the mind, without growing soft. Wealth we consider an opportunity for service, not something to brag about; poverty, no disgrace for any man to confess—the disgrace lies in not working to escape it. Among us, too, the same men direct both their own business and affairs of state, and working men form a very adequate judgment on politics. We alone call the man who takes no part in these things not 'quiet' but 'useless,' and we ourselves personally either decide policy or at least form a sound judgment on it; for we do not consider that debate makes action ineffective, but rather that the practice of rushing into action without being informed beforehand does so. Indeed, we surpass others in this, too, that we who run the risks are the very same men who weigh up the chances of an operation; whereas

[2] E.g. the Athenian pottery that decks modern museums.

among others, ignorance brings boldness, while reflection results in hesitation. But those men surely should be deemed bravest, who know most clearly what danger is and what pleasure is, and are not thereby made to flinch.

". . . In a word, I claim that our city as a whole is an education to Greece, and that our individual citizens excel all men in brilliant quickness of wit and self-reliance in action. That this is not a mere boast for this occasion, but actual truth, let the power of our city bear witness!—a power gained by the character that I have described. We alone in the day of trial prove greater than our reputation; we alone give our assailant no cause to complain at being beaten by 'men like those,' nor our subjects to feel shame at being under unworthy masters. Great are the memorials of our power; there is no lack of evidence of it, to bear us witness both to-day and for the admiration of generations to come. We have no need of Homer to praise us, nor of any poet, whose words give pleasure for a moment, but whose fictions are put to shame by the truth; but we have laid open by our daring every sea and land, and everywhere left the lasting imprint of our services or our revenges.

"Such is the City for which these men, making the hero's choice, that she should not be taken from them, died in battle; and for all of us who are left it is only natural that every man should be ready to spend himself for her. That is why I have dwelt so long upon the City: to show that we have more at stake than men who have no such heritage, and to support by proofs my eulogy of the men over whom I am now speaking. Indeed, I have now given you the chief points of that eulogy; for all those things, for which I sang the praise of our City, were the work of these brave men and of others like them.

"There are not many men whose achievements, like theirs, really match all that can be said of them; but I believe that a death like this shows a man's worth, whether it be the first visible noble action or the last in a noble life. For even of those whose past lives were less good, it is just and fair to remember their gallantry on behalf of their country in face of the enemy; they have blotted out

evil with good, and done more of service to the City than
ever they did of harm in their private lives. Not one of
these shrank back, either from the rich man's desire to
enjoy his wealth longer or from the poor man's hope to
escape his poverty; but they counted this the noblest danger, and a blow at their country's enemies dearer than
life. They left to the unknown future the question of success or failure and trusted in their own hands for the work
that lay before them now. So in the shock of battle,
choosing to die rather than save themselves by hanging
back, they feared dishonour and not the physical danger,
and in a moment, at the very culmination of glory rather
than of terror, passed away.

"Thus, worthily of the City, these men bore themselves;
and we who are left may pray to be spared their extreme
trial, but must disdain to show a less valiant spirit—thinking not only of all the hackneyed phrases that one might
repeat about the reasons for defending one's country, but
of the visible splendour of our City, seen day by day. May
Athens be the passion of our lives, and when you consider how great she is, think of this too: that all this was
gained by men, who faced danger and knew their duty
and shunned dishonour, and, if they met with defeat did
not think that any reason for giving up, but offered themselves as the fairest sacrifice that they could make for her.
They gave their lives for their country and won for themselves a fame that shall not grow old, and the finest
sepulchre that can be—not only that in which their bodies
are laid, but in the memories of men, among whom, when
any crisis calls for speech or action, their fame shall live
for ever.

"For the whole earth is the sepulchre of famous men,
and that fame remains not only on graven tablets in their
homeland, but also, unwritten, in lands not theirs—the
memory of their spirit, not of their fate. Emulate them,
therefore, and believing that Happiness is Freedom, and
Freedom, Courage, do not shun the dangers of battle. For
it is not the miserable man who should be most unsparing
of his life, but the fortunate ones, who have most to lose
by defeat. To be humbled through one's own cowardice is

more painful to a man of spirit than a quick death, when still full of strength and confidence, among one's comrades.

"Therefore I do not weep for the parents of the dead who are with us to-day, but will comfort them. They know into what a world of changes and chances we are born; and the happiest are they who win an honourable death, like these men, or an honourable sorrow like yours, and who do not live on till they have outlived their prosperity. I know that it is not easy to convince you of this— seeing the happiness of others, you will be reminded so often of that which once was yours; and grief is not felt for the lack of good things that one has never known, but of those that one has lost after learning to rely on them. Yet you must endure, in the hope of other children, those who are still of an age to bear them, and they will help to fill the gap. But those of you who are past the prime of life, count it gain that your time of happiness has been the longer and what remains will be short; and lighten your grief by thinking of the fair renown of the dead. For the love of honour is the only thing that does not weaken with age; and the old man's helplessness is most cheered, not by riches as some say, but by being looked upon with honour.

"To you children and brothers of the fallen, I say: there is a hard struggle in front of you; for all men praise the dead; so you will have to try your hardest if you are to be thought—not as good as they, but even only little inferior.

"If I must speak also of the glory of women, to those who are now made widows, I can sum up all in brief: It is great glory for you not to fall short of the nature that is in you, and to be spoken of by men as little as possible, either in praise or blame.

"My words are done, to the best of my ability and in obedience to the law. As a practical tribute, these whom we are burying have received our offerings now, and the state will look after their children till they are of age, thinking it good to hold out this prize, both for these men and for those who are left, for such a contest. For where excellence is best rewarded, there are the best citizens found.

"And now, when you have finished mourning those dear to you, it is time to depart."

Pericles idealises some things, no doubt; what funeral oration does not? For example, money, as well as birth, certainly "talked" in Athenian society. "Do you, *a poor man,* dare" (to criticise the state)? the chorus of Acharnians ask the old antiwar peasant in Aristophanes. But it is all very Athenian; not least, the bleakness of Pericles' "comfort" for the parents and widows of the dead. Perhaps only in the heyday of Athens could a statesman at a public funeral have dared to be so unsentimental and so austere. Especially characteristic are the words on the glory of a woman, which show up in a dry light the most fundamental weakness in Athenian civilisation. The Athenian and Ionian keeping of women uneducated and almost in "purdah" was one of the points on which Plato, that magnificent if reactionary rebel, knew better. So did Sparta, whose girls ran and wrestled, and whose women administered property and were fit companions at least for Spartans. So, one would have thought, did Aspasia's lover; but a state funeral was not the occasion on which to say so.

The winter passed, to the accompaniment of much business in the shipyards of Piræus. Athenian ingenuity was coping with the problem of transporting cavalry by sea in appreciable numbers and landing them on a beach —a problem quite as serious as that of landing tanks nowadays, and solved similarly, by the provision of novel, specialised craft. By the spring a sufficient number of the new horse-transports were ready; old ships specially converted.

Spring came, with the swallows and the corn and, in due course, the Peloponnesians. Once again the peasants of Attica streamed into the town; and then something happened which made mock of all Pericles' plans for a relatively bloodless war.

Chapter 14

The Plague

THE PELOPONNESIANS had not been long in Attica when plague was reported from Piræus. The rumour spread that Peloponnesian agents had poisoned the cisterns; but then the sickness spread to the upper city as well, where there was running water. Better-informed people connected it with the pestilence that, starting in "Ethiopia, beyond Egypt," had already ravaged much of the Persian Empire. It was terribly hot in the over-crowded city. The seasonal north winds failed almost completely that year, and the huts of the refugees stank to heaven. But in spite of a mounting death-rate, preparations for the summer sea-raid went on.

Archidamos, having "felt" the defence in the previous summer and made sure that Pericles would not fight, this year led down his main army to devastate the plain of Athens. Thence, leaving ruin behind, they moved on eastwards, past Hymettos, and raided right down the peninsula into the silver-mining district. While they were there, at their farthest point from home, Pericles himself set sail, with a hundred Athenian triremes, fifty from Lesbos and Chios, 4,000 Athenian armoured infantry, and 300 cavalry in the new horse-transports, and struck straight across the gulf to attack the considerable city of Epidauros.

Epidauros, as a Spartan ally, must have sent a contingent to Attica, and was thinly garrisoned. Pericles' sudden assault, delivered in great strength, very nearly captured it; but not quite. Surprise being thus lost, it was useless to settle down to a siege; a blockade would soon be interrupted by the return of the main Peloponnesian army; so after devastating the country, the expedition set sail again, rounded the peninsula of Argolis, harrying the coasts of Troizen and Hermione, crossed the Argolic Gulf to sack Prasiai on the coast of Lakonia, and so returned home.

This episode shows that Pericles' advice to the Assembly, "not to try to extend the empire during the war," did not mean that Athens was not to hit back hard against the Peloponnese—so long only as she did not endanger her main forces. It referred rather to purely divergent operations in distant regions like Sicily. The strategic effects of the capture of Epidauros would have been far-reaching. The walled city, once taken and its people perhaps ejected, would not have been hard to hold; and its territory marched with that of neutral and friendly Argos. Troizen and Hermione would have been isolated and probably won over; Athens would have had a firmer footing in the Peloponnese than before 446, and the position of Corinth would have been serious.

Pericles returned to find the plague raging at Athens, with an alarming death-roll. The Spartans had gone—scared away, some said, by the news brought by runaway slaves and by the smoke which they could see rising from many funeral pyres; but they had stayed in the country for forty days, the longest, as it proved, of all their invasions. As the 4,000 men of the expeditionary force were now free, it was decided to send them to Poteidaia, under Hagnon and Kleopompos, to try by a full-dress assault with battering-rams to end the long and expensive blockade. The result, however, was disastrous; they carried the plague with them, and communicated it to the troops already there; and in camp conditions the death-rate was even higher than in Athens. After six weeks, Hagnon called off the campaign and, leaving a blockading force as before, returned to Athens, having lost by sickness alone 1,050 men.

The great Plague of Athens seems to have been, in its primary and generally deadly manifestations, pneumonic (the form which the Black Death assumed in France, after appearing in the bubonic form in Italy). Thucydides, who himself suffered from it, describes it with the stern accuracy of a scientific report, conscientiously avoiding the loose speculation as to causes and origins in which "both doctors and untrained people," as he drily remarks, were indulging all round him. Individuals in perfect health would be seized suddenly with violent headaches: the eyes were bloodshot, the tongue and gullet red, the breath foul and noisome. Then came sneezing, hoarseness, and shortly afterwards violent coughing, and "retching of every kind of bile known to medical science, accompanied by great distress. . . . The body was not hot to the touch, nor pale, but flushed and livid, breaking out in a rash of small ulcers and pustules; but internally there was such burning fever that the patient could not bear the covering of even the thinnest clothes or sheets, or anything else than to be absolutely naked; and the great wish was to throw oneself into cold water. Many, being untended, did so, into the wells, consumed as they were with thirst; but it made no difference however much one drank. And the distress of insomnia was upon one all this time." Death came usually either about the seventh to the ninth day from the fever, or else later from ulceration of the stomach, diarrhœa, and general exhaustion. Of those who recovered, some did so relatively quickly after the fever and cough had gone, some slowly or not completely at all; "for the plague went through the whole body from the head downwards, and if one survived the main attack, it fastened on the extremities." People survived with crippled hands or feet, or impotent, or blind, or with total loss of memory. "Even carrion-eating birds and beasts, though there were many corpses lying unburied, never went near them, or if they ate of them, they died. In fact, there was a conspicuous absence of such birds. In dogs, the result could naturally be better studied."

The infectiousness of the disease was appalling. Many doctors died. People caught it from those whom they were trying to nurse, until in the end people became afraid to go near the sick at all. Some houses were left empty, the whole family having died for lack of attention. Alternatively, those who did attend to the sick died off; "especially," say Thucydides grimly, "the most virtuous; for their sense of honour made them unsparing of themselves in visiting friends whose own kin had given them up at last, overborne by the greatness of the disaster. Those who had recovered, however, took pity on the sick and dying, because they knew the disease already, and because they themselves were in safety; for the plague never attacked the same person twice, at least not fatally. Such people were the object of congratulations, and they themselves felt a sort of superstitious confidence that no disease was ever going to kill them after that."

This evidently was how Thucydides, austere, conscientious, and a man of wide human sympathies, gained his detailed knowledge of the endless variations of the disease.

The plague lasted all that summer, and the next, and after a pause in 428 flared up again finally in 427. Three hundred knights, 4,400 of the middle-class armoured spearmen registered on the War Office lists, died in all; of the poor, probably an even higher proportion. Thucydides, as he went about his self-imposed duties, noted the growing signs of social disintegration. The refugees in their stifling shacks died off (like Hagnon's men in camp) even faster than those who had proper houses. The dead and dying lay on top of each other, or sprawled in the streets and round all the springs. There were corpses in the temples where they had been camping; what would before the war have been a shocking sacrilege had ceased to attract attention. People disposed of their dead "anyhow one could," often regardless of decency; sometimes putting a corpse upon someone else's pyre and setting a light to it, or throwing a second body on top of one that was already burning, and running away.

Demoralisation took the form of a general outbreak of hedonism. Pleasure-seeking became more fevered, vice more unblushing, the desire for quick profits keener, the will to take trouble for an ideal almost non-existent; while "religion and law alike lost their power to restrain; religion, because men saw the pious and the irreligious perishing alike, and law, because they felt that they would probably not live long enough to be brought to book for their misdeeds, as a worse doom hung over the heads of all and before it fell it was reasonable to get some pleasure out of life." The picture is extraordinarily like that in

Boccaccio, of Florentine society under the shadow of the Black Death.

In the circumstances it was hardly surprising that the people turned upon Pericles as the author of their misfortunes. They even, perhaps during his absence with the fleet, made overtures for peace; but the Spartans stood out for terms that the ambassadors had no power to accept. They returned to Athens, and Pericles, finding himself the object of the people's despairing rage, demanded an Assembly, to defend himself and attack those who sued for peace at such a moment.

"I am not surprised at your anger," Thucydides reports him, "for I know its cause. That is why I have called this meeting—to remind you of certain facts, and to find fault with you for what is illogical in your anger with me and your attitude of defeatism." They must, he goes on, set the state's well-being above their individual troubles; for if the state fares well it can look after its less fortunate citizens, but if his country falls, no individual's prosperity can survive.

He demands, in effect, a vote of confidence, as an adviser of well-tried judgment, patriotism, and indifference to money. In blaming him, he points out, they blamed themselves for taking his advice in voting for war. If there had been any choice, it was lunacy to go to war; but if the only alternative was for the city to be at the mercy of its neighbours, then "the man who shirks the risk should be blamed, not he who faces it. I am the same man still, and have not shifted my position; it is you who change, since you were convinced by my reasoning when unhurt, and regret it when things go badly." They must not let their judgment be warped by the present unexpected and unpredictable disaster. He had explained at other times the reasons for confidence in final victory; but "here," he goes on, "is a new point, which I do not think you have realised, and which I myself have not mentioned in previous speeches."

This new point was the absolutely unlimited potentialities of Athens' unrivalled sea-power. The whole sea was theirs, not only so far as their ships now plied, but as much farther as they chose. There was, in fact, a very good reason why Pericles had never exploited it before. It was a very dangerous theme, for a people whose great fault was overconfidence. "I should not mention it now," went on Pericles frankly, "so daring it sounds, were it not for the excessive depression in which I see you."

They must not then be too distressed at the devastation of the land. They should think of their lands as an added amenity, not the basis of their wealth. "Make up your minds that if we hold fast our freedom" [our freedom of action, we should say] "we shall easily regain all this; but people who are dependent on others lose even the wealth they had."

Then comes an appeal to pride; not to be weaker than their fathers who gained and held the empire by their labours; pride in the empire itself. "You must support the city's reputation, which depends on this empire of which you are all proud. Either do not shirk the labour, or do not expect the glory. Realise, too, that you are fighting not only for one thing—freedom or subjection—but also to avert the loss of your empire, and the revenge of those who hate you for having had it. And *you cannot lay it down* (in case anyone who is now feeling frightened tries to make a virtue of 'peaceableness'); for this empire of yours is now a despotism, which it may have been wrong to acquire, but which it is now dangerous to let go. Gentry like these" [the peace party] "if people listen to them . . . are the quickest to ruin a city. Peaceableness cannot survive unless it is wedded to vigour in action; nor is it any virtue for an imperial city, but for subjects—a slave's virtue, to save his skin.

"Do not be led astray by people like these! And do not be angry with me, you who took with me the decision to fight, because the enemy have come and done exactly what they might be expected to do if you refused to submit, nor yet because of the present epidemic—the one factor in the present situation that was not anticipated. That, I know, is one reason for the feeling against me—which is very unfair, unless you are also going to credit me with any good luck that you may meet with! You must bear the acts of God with resignation, and of the state's enemies with courage; this was the way of Athens in the past; do not let it end with you. Remember that her name stands highest among all mankind because of her steadfastness in adversity and the blood and sweat that she has spent in wars, and that hers was the strongest power that has ever yet been seen; a power whose memory will remain for ever, even if we do now give in, as it is in the nature of things to decay; the memory that we ruled over more Greeks than any other Greek state, that we held our own in greater wars against them, whether severally or all together, and that ours was the greatest and best-found city of the world.

"These are things which the pacifist may condemn; but the man of action will admire them, and those who have no such power will envy. Unpopularity at the time has been the lot of every ruling power, and to accept it, for a great end, is the soundest attitude. The hatred does not last long; but the splendours of the hour and the glory that follows after are remembered for ever. Look then to your fair fame in the future, and to your honour now. Send no more heralds to Sparta, and let no one see you overwhelmed by your present troubles; but consider that those who meet trouble with the stoutest heart and the strongest hands are both the best citizens and the best individuals."

Pericles won his point, in so far as no more overtures were made to Sparta; but, humanly and illogically, the bitterness against him remained. His enemies seized their opportunity. Not long afterwards, for the first time in fifteen years, Pericles lost the position of general—perhaps suspended by the refusal of the vote of confidence which (at least in the next century) had to be passed in each prytany.

Suspension implied the immediate scrutiny of a general's accounts, with or without formal impeachment; it appears that Pericles' accounts were in confusion—hardly surprising in such a year—so that the Council inevitably had to find a true bill and send the case before the law courts. Drakontides, probably with hostile intent, carried a proposal that Pericles' account-books should be deposited with the Prytaneis; that the trial should take place on the holy ground of the Acropolis, and that the jury should take their voting ballots from the altar itself; but Hagnon (on his return from Thrace in July?) got this theatrical procedure amended. Pericles was tried before an ordinary jury of 1,501 (three panels of 500, grouped for this important case). He was found at fault to the extent of five talents—a modest sum in the circumstances —and fined, probably, fifteen.

Pericles now had an opportunity to rest, but he got little joy of it. The plague was at its height; almost every day brought news of the death of some friend or associate. Pericles' sister died; so did Xanthippos, still unreconciled to his father after their bitter quarrel; then, very shortly afterwards, Paralos, his only other legitimate son. When he followed the funeral of the young man, and the time came for him to lay a wreath upon the corpse, it was observed for the second time in his career that Pericles wept.

While he remained at home in mourning, it was represented to him that if he would stand again for the generalship, he would certainly be elected. The people had got over their resentment; many, probably, were ashamed of themselves; and his old colleagues were missing him at councils of war. Pericles had done with ambition; but his friends—among others Alkibiades, now a handsome, gallant, ambitious, young soldier—urged him, saying the city had need of him. He stood, and was elected. As a token of favour, and that his house might not be left without heirs, the Assembly also legitimised and "made an Athenian"—a step that now required such an Act of Parliament—Pericles' namesake, his natural son by Aspasia. It was one of the ironies of his career that Pericles, the author of the law of 451, should have to ask such a favour.

The younger Pericles lived to be a general (and, the financial records show, a prominent one) in the later years of the Peloponnesian War, before falling a victim in one of the last tragedies of that long-drawn struggle.

In 429, Pericles was elected general for the last time; but he leaves no further mark in the pages of Thucydides. He was a sick man; one of those, perhaps, who survived an attack of the plague, but never fully recovered. His absence was already affecting operations of war: for example, when reinforcements were being sent to Phormion, who with only twenty ships was on guard at Naupaktos, with the ambitious assignment of blocking the Corinthian Gulf. The enemy were mustering in overwhelming strength to destroy him; but the Assembly—no military expert, it seems, now strong enough to deter it—gave the reinforcements a mission to accomplish in Crete *on the way*. The result was that the squadron failed in Crete, and after being held there by north winds arrived too late at Naupaktos. That Phormion survived the attack was merely due to the superb skill and morale of himself and his sailors.

But Pericles lay bedridden. Aspasia—can one blame her?—was wondering who would protect her if he died. (She picked on the rising radical general Lysikles, but he was killed in action in winter 428–427. However, her son Pericles was growing up by 424.) To a friend who visited him, the old man showed something hanging by a string round his neck. "A charm!" said Pericles. "The women hung it on me. Eh, I must be in a poor way, when I put up with that sort of superstition!"

As the hot weather passed into the soft Greek autumn and the plague at length showed signs of abating, it became clear that he was dying. The room was full of generals, ex-generals, notabilities, and the survivors of his old friends, come to bid him farewell. We have no list of their names, but can make a good guess at many: tried colleagues like Hagnon and Nikias, who was to succeed him, so far as mediocrity can succeed genius; the fighting generals, like Lamachos and Phormion (back victorious from the west, to die soon after, probably of the plague); Thucydides, probably; Hipponikos, son of old Kallias and husband of Pericles' ex-wife; of the younger men, Alkibiades and Hippokrates, Pericles' brother's son, who was to attempt the reconquest of Boiotia and to meet his death there; the boy Pericles, shy and unsure of his position, and old Sophocles, who was to live and work in fullest possession of his faculties for another twenty-three years.

Pericles seemed unconscious, and they talked of his greatness and magnanimity and achievements, including no less than nine trophies set up for victories won under his command. But the brain that had been for so long the brain of Athens had not yet ceased working, and a whisper from the bed interrupted them. Pericles said he was surprised that they talked of victories—things that depended largely on fortune, and had happened to many generals. "But you have not spoken," he said, "of the best thing: that is, that no Athenian ever wore mourning because of me."

So died the great builder and idealist, leaving his city beset by war and the plague, and with no one fit to succeed him as adviser to the democracy. He could withstand the people to their face so that, Thucydides says, "it was democracy in theory, but the rule of the chief citizen in practice. But his successors, being more on a level with each other, and rivals for power, tried to please the people by giving way to them. And from that arose many mistakes. . . ."

Even apart from that, Pericles' peculiar blend of military and political strategy made him a dangerous model to imitate. The political general is traditionally a bad general. That Pericles himself met with no disasters was due to the fact that he always aimed, during his period of supremacy, at strictly limited objectives, as well as to his combining, like Marlborough, political and military power. Nikias, a hard-working, methodical brigadier, who feared only the people, imitated Pericles' caution and attention to details, with an infinite capacity for taking pains, but without genius, and avoided disaster for as long as Demos allowed him, by avoiding major actions altogether. Alkibiades, who became a general at thirty, was far more dangerous; he was continually trying to achieve by diplomacy conquests that could only be won by hard fighting if at all; misunderstanding Pericles, whose strategy, in the years when Alkibiades remembered him, had served a policy not of extending Athens' power but of conserving it.

The war dragged on, growing increasingly bitter, as the latent class-war in the Greek states burst into flame in city after city, the democrats everywhere inclining to Athens and the oligarchs to Sparta. Thucydides analyses, with merciless lucidity, the neuroses of war and revolution and the increasing success of the cruder types of intelligence in these conditions. Athens was still strong enough to suppress revolts in the Empire, and did so, with increasing brutality; but her counter-blows at the main enemy lacked weight since the plague, and were mostly failures. A gallant and attractive Spartan, Brasidas, with very small forces, made his way overland to Thrace, where he captured Amphipolis and spread rebellion in Chalkidike. And yet even so, Athens weathered the storm: after ten years of desultory war, a peace, the Peace of Nikias, was concluded leaving both sides to hold what they had at the time. It would have been well if that were the end of the story; but now comes forward the brilliant, unstable, ambitious Alkibiades, a heaven-sent leader for the war-party—for the trading classes for whom war had become a profession. Led by Alkibiades, Athens plunged into a policy of adventures; took a nasty knock in an attempt to back Argos in a land war with Sparta; slaughtered the whole male population of Melos island, which refused to join her empire; and then embarked on the wildest aggression of all, against Syracuse.

Nikias opposed this project, as unsound, but he was not strong enough to resist the people to the end, and ultimately found himself in charge of it. Alkibiades was in joint command; and then his enemies felled him with a prosecution for sacrilege, for courting the anger of heaven against Athens by a wild parody of the Holy Mysteries of Eleusis, in which he and some friends had indulged at a drunken party. Alkibiades fled to Sparta, and gave advice that was ruinous to his own country.

Nikias' army in Sicily was baffled, defeated, cut off, and at last utterly destroyed. It was the decisive blow. Though she struggled on grimly for another ten long years, against renewed Peloponnesian attacks, Athens fell at last, her fleet destroyed, her empire in revolt, her city besieged and starving. Even her democracy was overthrown, though for a few months only.

With Alkibiades indeed the curse of the Alkmeonidai came home. Where Pericles, bred in an older world, had devoted every natural gift to the service of Athens, and had desired to rule her (so at least he would have rationalised) only that he might serve, Alkibiades, growing up in Pericles' strange house and in an age of intellectual disintegration, quite consciously sought to enjoy himself, even in politics. He, above all, though among many others, was the fated instrument by which Athens came to disaster.

And yet, after all, Pericles' objects were only those of every other Athenian imperialist, though his methods showed greater prudence. He had laboured, often for peace, always to conserve Athens' strength; but he recoiled, it seems, only *pour mieux sauter*. No doubt, if he had died young, someone else would have led Athens on the paths of empire, and probably done it worse. But as things were, it is he above all others who was identified with the growth of the Athenian Empire, leading Athens ever farther into the impasse, ever higher above her subject "allies," to an ever more dangerous and lonely eminence.

This brings us back to his last recorded words. "No Athenian ever wore black because of me." He was thinking, no doubt, of his carefulness of his men's lives in the field and of his magnanimity and liberalism at home. But can he really have believed that no wives and mothers of the men who fell in the war which he, against opposition, had precipitated had "worn black because of him"? Or had the dying Pericles an uneasy conscience, and did the idealist within him know that in his work for the supremacy of Athens, and for his own supremacy *in* Athens, he had been even as all the older Alkmeonidai?

For, indeed, that great house was truly under a curse, if we may accept what the wise man of Ephesos said. "A man's Dæmon" [his guardian spirit, and so his fate] "is his character," said Herakleitos; and the leading trait in the character of all the great Alkmeonids, whether they conspired with a tyrant or against him, whether they founded a democracy or described it like Alkibiades as "patent lunacy," was the craving to be first. It was rare, as a result, for an Alkmeonid to end his life without disaster; and if we say with Herakleitos that a man's Character is his Fate, we may well add that the unquiet mind of the dying Perikles, the noblest of their line, was the avenging Fury of the House of Alkmeon.

Genealogical Table

SOME FAMILIES OF
THE ATHENIAN ARISTOCRACY

To illustrate their influence and their marriage alliances under the Periclean democracy.

| PHILAIDAI | ALKMEONIDAI | HERALDS | (PHILAIDAI?) | HERALDS |

HERALDS

Andokides, Treasurer of Athene, 6th cent.
(?)
Leogoras, General against Peisistratos, 546
X
ANDOKIDES, General, 446, 441, Ambassador, 445, etc. — Leogoras
D. m. Andokides, 302, Ambassador, famous orator

(PHILAIDAI?)

Epilykos
Teisandros (pp. 119, 126)
Epilykos, d. 415 in Sicily — D. m.
Leagros m. D.

HERALDS

Hipponikos (made money on Solon's reforms)
Phainippos (?)
Kallias
Hipponikos the Rich ("Ammon")
KALLIAS, Ambassador, 449, 445, etc.
Hipponikos, General, 426 — married — D.
Kallias m. D., General, 390, Ambassador, 372

Glaukon
Leagros the Handsome, General, d. 465
Glaukon, General, 441, 433 m. D. — D. m.

ALKMEONIDAI

Megakles "the Accused," Archon, c. 632
Alkmeon, General, c. 590
Agariste m. (c. 570) Megakles
Kleisthenes the Law-Giver — D. (?) m. Megakles
Megakles — m a r r i e d — Agariste m. Xanthippos, General, 479
Ariphron
Hippokrates

PERICLES — m. (1) X who m. (2)
Xanthippos
Pericles, General, 429–406
PERICLES m. (2) Aspasia

ALKIBIADES m. Hipparete, General, 420, 415, 408, etc.
Deinomache m. Kleinias (pp. 101–9)
Kleinias, sub-normal
Other sons

PHILAIDAI

Kypselos, Tyrant of Corinth
D. m. — Teisandros
Hippokleides "the Suitor" (p. 4), Archon 566
Kypselos
Kypselos — m. X Stesagoras
Miltiades, Tyrant of Chersonese
Oloros, a Prince of Thrace
Hegesipyle — m. (2) — m. MILTIADES of Marathon m. (1) X
Kimon "the Idiot", race-horse owner — X m. Stesagoras
Miltiades, Archon, c. 659

KIMON m. (1) X
Elpinike — m a r r i e d — (2) Isodike
Euryptolemos (p. 59)
D. (?)
Lakedaimonios, General, 433
Oloros
Hegesipyle m. Oloros
THOUKYDIDES, General, 424; Historian
Thoukydides (pp. 104–124) m. D.

Note on Books

Note on Books

I. Biographies

E. Abbott, *Pericles,* in *Heroes of the Nations* Series (Putnam, New York and London, 1891) (very critical).

Compton Mackenzie, *Pericles* (Hodder and Stoughton, London, 1937) (laudatory).

II. Histories of Greece

Still readable and often illuminating is that of the 19th-century liberal, George Grote (1st edn., 12 vols., John Murray, 1849; also in Everyman's Library, 12 vols.; both often found second-hand). Vols. V and VI cover the lifetime of Pericles. The one-volume edition by Mitchell and Caspari (Max Cary) brings in the results of modern discovery down to about 1910.

The best, substantial one-volume history, giving reference to sources, is still:

J. B. Bury, *A History of Greece,* ed. 3 by Russell Meiggs, 1951.

This deals thoroughly with political and military history, but only secondarily with other aspects of culture.

M. L. W. Laistner, *A History of the Greek World, 476-323* B.C., 1936.

Sir Alfred Zimmern, *The Greek Commonwealth,* Galaxy Books, 1962 gives an attractive if slightly idealised picture of Athens.

C. E. Robinson, *A History of Greece,* 1929, shorter than the above, is an attractive and well-illustrated school-book.

The Cambridge Ancient History, Vol. V, Athens, is rather disappointing, but includes distinguished chapters, VII, by Sir F. Adcock, and XV, on Art, by Sir John Beazley.

See also *Athenian Democracy,* by A. H. M. Jones (1957).

III. Art and Archæology

The Ancient City of Athens, by Ida Thallon Hill (1953) incorporates the important additions to knowledge made by the American excavations. See also *The Athenian Agora,* a guide to the excavations, by Mabel Lang and C. W. J. Eliot (American School of Classical Studies at Athens, 1954).

Everyday Things in Greece, by M. and C. H. B. Quennell (1932) is a handy introduction to its subject.

Among illustrated books may be mentioned:

The Athenian Acropolis, by Hege and Rodenwaldt (Eng. trn., 1930).

Greek Architecture, by A. W. Lawrence (Pelican History of Art, 1956).

The Sculpture of the Parthenon, by P. E. Corbett (King Penguin, 1959).

IV. Sources in Translation

Thucydides: tr. A. de Selincourt (Penguin Classics); by Sir Richard Livingstone, slightly abridged, in *World's Classics* (Oxford U.P.); older trn. by R. Crawley (Everyman; also Bohn's Classical Library), often found secondhand.

Aristotle (?) *Constitution of Athens:* tr. F. G. Kenyon (Bell, 1904).

"*The Old Oligarch*": tr. by J. A. Petch (Blackwell, Oxford, 1926). (Also found in translations of Xenophon's works, e.g. in Bohn.)

Plutarch's *Lives:* numerous translations. The Athenian Lives are now collected in Ian Scott-Kilvert's *The Rise and Fall of Athens* (Penguin Classics, 1960).

The Introduction to A. W. Gomme's *Commentary on Thucydides,* Vol. I, pp. 1-87, contains an admirable discussion of all these sources, especially Plutarch (pp. 54-84).

V. Inscriptions

Inscriptions (nearly always mutilated) cannot be studied without a considerable knowledge of Greek. The best introduction is M. N. Tod, *Greek Historical Inscriptions* (Oxford U.P., 2nd ed., 1946). Essential for advanced study is *Athenian Tribute-Lists* by Meritt, Wade-Gery and McGregor; in all major libraries.

VI. Articles

Brilliant, and of especial importance, are those of Wade-Gery on "Thucydides the Son of Melesias" and on "The Peace of Kallias" (both now in his *Essays in Greek History,* Blackwell, Oxford, 1958); also "The Question of Tribute in 449-8", in *Hesperia,* XIV (1945); cf. Meritt and Hill, "The Decree of Kleinias", *ib.* XIII (1944). See also:

R. Meiggs, "The Development of the Athenian Empire", in *Journal of Hellenic Studies,* LXIII.

A. E. Taylor, "The Dates of the Attacks on Pericles' Friends", in *Classical Quarterly,* XI (1917).

INDEX

Index

Casual references are not indexed in the following columns. Under "Athens" only references to the town itself are indexed; for other aspects of Athenian life see "Constitution," "Navy," etc.